1,001 RECRUIT TIPS: *COLLEGE COACHES EDITION*

RECRUITING MADE SIMPLE

WRITTEN BY: @1001RECRUITTIPS

No part of this publication may be reproduced, stored in a retrieval system or transmitted in any form or by any means, electronic, mechanical, photocopying, recording, scanning or otherwise.

This publication is an independent information source not approved, recommended, associated with or prepared by the NCAA, NAIA or any individual coach or university.

Trademarks: NCAA is a trademark or registered trademark of The National Collegiate Athletic Association. All trademarks are the property of their respective owners.

LIMIT OF LIABILITY/DISCLAIMER OF WARRANTY: The publisher and the author make no representations or warranties with respect to the accuracy or completeness of the contents of this work and specifically disclaim all warranties , including without limitation warranties of fitness for a particular purpose. No warranty may be created or extended by sales or promotional materials, the advice and strategies contained herein may not be suitable for every situation. This work is sold with the understanding that the publisher is not engaged in rendering legal, accounting, or other professional services. If professional assistance is required, the services of a competent professional person should be sought, neither the publisher nor the author shall be liable for damages arising herefrom, the fact that an organization or website is referred to in this work as a citation and/or a potential source of further information does not mean that the author or the publisher endorses the information the organization or website may provide or recommendations it may make, further, readers should be aware that internet websites listed in this work may have changed or disappeared between when this work was written and when it is read.

Text Copyright © 2016 All Rights Reserved

All rights reserved. ISBN-10:0-9859048-6-0
ISBN-13:978-0-9859048-6-9

TO ALL OF THE OUTSTANDING COACHING MENTORS AND PLAYERS THAT I'VE BEEN ABLE TO LEARN FROM.... THANK YOU FOR LETTING ME BE A PART OF SUCH TRADITIONS, THE DAILY LAUGHS AND CHAMPIONSHIP (AND NOT SO CHAMPIONSHIP) RUNS!

TABLE OF CONTENTS

CHAPTER #1 — 8 WAYS TO DISCOVER PLAYERS
No Stone Left Unturned..14
8 Ways to Discover Players..15
8 Ways to Discover Players: Scouting Services...15
8 Ways to Discover Players: Regional or National Combines....................16
8 Ways to Discover Players: Tournaments and Games..............................17
8 Ways to Discover Players: Prep Recommendations................................19
8 Ways to Discover Players: Camps...21
8 Ways to Discover Players: Highlight Videos..23
8 Ways to Discover Players: Were Offered By Rival.................................... 25
8 Ways to Discover Players: Political Referrals..25

CHAPTER #2 — GATHERING INFO
Importance of Great Data...28
Organized Across the Board..29
Keep Everything..32
Distance From Home...33
Questionnaires..34
Nicknames or Preferred Names...35
Scouting Reports & AAU Packets..35
Phone Calls..36
Social Media..36
High School Coach Database...38
Stay Updated on Prospect News...38

CHAPTER #3 - EVALUATIONS
Responsibilities as a Staff...40
Building Your Watch List of Prospects..42
Transfers and JuCo Players..44
Gathering Video..45
Time Management Before Watching Prospect's Video..............................45
Fit for Head Coach...47
How to Be a Great Evaluator of Talent - Qualities to Look For..................47
Ranking Your Watch List...49
Evaluating Intangibles..51
Evaluating Risk vs. Reward...52
Building a Team...54
Scholarship Offers..55
Can They Be Successful Within the Current System, Program and University? 55
Do They Really Want to Be Here? 56
Travel Plans...56

CHAPTER #4 - ACADEMICS

Know SAT/ACT Dates..60
Your Players Improve..60
Understanding Your University Admissions Policies.................................62
Understanding Your University Academic Selling Points..........................63
Likelihood of Graduation...64
Involve University Faculty Members..64
Scholarship Breakdown of Needed Academic Requirements.....................65

CHAPTER #5 – RECRUITING CYCLE

Year-to-Year..68
Yearly Schedule...72
Taking Over a New Job...72
Keeping Up With Latest Technology...77
Official and Unofficial Visit Planning...78
Changing Minds...80
Self-Evaluate with Current Players..81
Player Host Decisions..82
Signing Day...82
Preparing for Enrollment...83

CHAPTER #6 - RELATIONSHIPS

Know People By Name..86
Your Own Family...88
Program Leaders..89
Your Current Players..90
Families of Current Players...91
Commits...91
Recruits with Special Needs..92
Parents of Recruits...92
Prep Coaches..96
High School Staffers..99
Assistant Coaches on Your Staff..100
Athletic Department...101
Your Office Staff..103
Your Compliance Office..105
University Student Body..105
Community and Fans...106
Former Players...106
Other College Coaches..109
The Pros...110
Rituals..111

CHAPTER #7 – SELLING YOUR PROGRAM

Target Audiences...114
Decision Makers..116
Top 30 Factors that Players and Families Consider 116
Tips for Conversations..117
What Parents Are Interested In..121
Daily List of Tasks...122
Mission Statement..123
3 Ways You Want Program to Be Thought Of....................................124
Control the Message...125
Academics...125
Promote the Head Coach..126
Developing and Marketing Your Selling Points..................................126
    - Selling Points..126
    - 180 Ways to Market Your Program...128
    - Quotes..132
    - Picture Library..132
    - Graphic Design..133
Master File of Selling Points...135
All-Department Marketing Meeting...135
Pageantry of Program...135
Time to Build..137
Official Visits...137
Unofficial Visits...140
Campus Tours...142
Key Pictures in Office...145
Be Prepared to Answer Questions...146
Leadership Development and Community Service............................150
Attendance..151
Celebrations..151
Gold Star Players..152
Legends of Program..153
Campus Safety..153
Negative Recruiting..154
Responding to Correspondence...155
Great Video Staff..155

CHAPTER #8 – SELLING YOURSELF
Winning..158
Develop Players...159
Simple, Proven Strategy..160
Analytics..161
Genuine Personality..162
Qualities of Successful Coaches..163
Qualities of Successful Recruiters...164
3 Ways You Want to Be Thought Of......................................165
Energy...165
Do Something Never Done Before..166
Keep Everything..166
Help of Spouse..167
Your Office..167
Quotes from Others...168

CHAPTER #9 - PERSONALITIES
Team Chemistry...170
Range of Staff Personalities..171
Admit Mistakes..172
Don't Be Caught Off-Guard...173
Never Bring a Bad Day to the Office.....................................174
Calm, Cool and Collected..175
Personal Life..175

CHAPTER #10 – SUPPORT STAFF
Administrative Assistants, Grad Assistants & Interns............178

CHAPTER #11 – ADVICE FOR HEAD COACHES
Advice to Become a Great Head Coach................................182
A 'No' Person...183
Self-Scout..183
Streamline...184
Keep Moving the Bar...185

CHAPTER #12 - ADVICE FOR ASSISTANT COACHES
Master Your Position...188
More Tips for Assistant Coaches...189

CHAPTER #13 - ADVICE FOR GRAD ASSISTANTS
Listen to Recruiting Calls..194
More Tips for Grad Assistants...194

RECRUITING BOILS DOWN TO A FEW THINGS— CREATING A VISION THAT PLAYERS WANT TO BE A PART OF, PROVIDING THE BEST OPPORTUNITY FOR THE PLAYER AND MOST IMPORTANTLY, TRUST AND GREAT RELATIONSHIPS.

There is no truer statement than, "Winning cures everything," especially in recruiting. So as much as your job is to recruit (often "selling a dream," getting players to buy into your vision before it's a reality)... your job will ultimately depend on your win-loss record. Never lose sight of this!

To fans, recruiting seems like a cut and dry job—make a few phone calls, fly out to some games and tournaments, host some Official Visits and let the opportunity of playing for their beloved university sell itself. After that, just sit back and collect those signed NLIs. After all, you have scholarships to offer, sometimes valuing over $200,000 – how hard can it be? "Why can't you bring in better players, we have so much to offer!" they'll say. Well, so do more than 1,300 college athletic programs out there and you're all basically selling similar opportunities: an education, playing time, a college family environment. You have to find ways to separate yourself!

Winning will be your biggest recruiting tool – so for this reason time management is critical. Yes, all coaches need to devote hours into recruiting calls, evaluating prospects videos, Official/Unofficial Visits, weeks on the road recruiting. But you also need to invest quality time into developing your players, gameplanning, scouting opponents, self-scouting and perfecting your "Core Winning Philosophies." You need to master the fine art of finding a way to win: both on-the-field and on the recruiting road.

Recruiting—as done by the best in the business – is an every day, every minute job. As much as you dream of being a successful coach, you will need to be a relentless recruiter.

From my experiences, excellent time management is one of the consistent traits that great coaches share. They prioritize time to game plan, and only invest their time in a few key areas.

From this day on you need to focus as much work time as possible on:
- **#1- ON-FIELD/COURT RESULTS**
- **#2- YOUR GAME AND PRACTICE PREPARATIONS**
- **#3- RECRUITING**
- **#4- RELATIONSHIPS WITH CURRENT PLAYERS / TEAM CHEMISTRY**

Sections of this book speak to the obvious recruiting topics: evaluations, offer procedures, academic requirements. But some topics may not seem related to recruiting: building relationships within the Athletic Department, your current player's academic improvements, your personal life, interns... but believe me, the greatest recruiters look at every detail of their program, their position, their life and their day and ask, "How can this impact recruiting?" How can you use any program detail to an advantage? Or, how can any of these details negatively impact your efforts? How can you find an edge as a program?

Sections of this book speak to coaches who have unlimited manpower and financial resources. Other tips can be applied by just changing a few of your daily routines, requiring zero budget! Cultures within every sport are different, not every section may apply to you. But, having worked within several levels, sports and budgets, understand that your budget plays a small role in comparison to your work ethic, personality and genuine love for the profession.

From this day forward, always make decisions within your program based on the impacts that will be felt with recruiting. What decisions can be made within your program that can ultimately help you recruit better athletes to your program?

> **"DON'T JUDGE EACH DAY BY THE HARVEST YOU REAP BUT BY THE SEEDS THAT YOU PLANT."**
> **-ROBERT LOUIS STEVENSON**

And, as an individual with career aspirations, make decisions based on the long-term vision of your future. You may not currently be at your dream school (and you may not get there for another decade or longer), so as you are making decisions and taking actions now, always be laser-focused on the big picture and where you want to go.

Some of the best advice I have heard along the way is, "Treat your current job as your dream job." Work just as hard and creatively in your current position as you would if you if you just took a job at your dream school. Protect your current position as you would if you were the head coach at your dream school. Treat your current job as the biggest opportunity of your life!

Exhaust every channel, become a master of time management. Focus on making friends along the way, get to know as many people as possible. All roads can lead you to the next great difference-maker for your program and career!

CHAPTER #1
8 WAYS TO DISCOVER PLAYERS

"Seek opportunities to show you care. The smallest gestures often make the biggest difference."
-JOHN WOODEN

"Leaders think and talk about the solutions. Followers think and talk about the problems."
-BRIAN TRACY

"Leaders are called to discover the hidden, encourage the uncertain, develop the untrained and empower the powerless."
-JOHN C. MAXWELL

"A man can be as great as he wants to be. If you believe in yourself and have the courage, the determination, the dedication, the competitive drive and if you are willing to sacrifice the little things in life and pay the price for the things that are worthwhile, it can be done.""
-VINCE LOMBARDI

8 WAYS TO DISCOVER PLAYERS: NO STONE LEFT UNTURNED

One of the most common questions or concerns that I hear from prospects is, "Help, I live in the middle of nowhere, coaches will never find me!" or "My team sucks, coaches will never come to my school to scout me." From my experience, this is one of the biggest misconceptions out there! The greatest recruiters I've learned from know that they must leave no stone unturned when searching for prospects, they work their relationships and trusted contacts to find some great hidden gems. Having great relationships with prep coaches and this "no stone left unturned" mindset can help you separate yourself as a recruiter!

It is for this reason that you need to recruit a great network of contacts around you -- prep coaches, scouting services, former players, alumni, principals, guidance counselors. You need trusted associates who will want to pick up the phone and call you to give you an early lead on a top local prospect. The greatest recruiters have a reputation as a coach that you can trust, so prep sources were always picking up the phone to tip them off on a young player before the masses of other college coaches came calling. Most prep coaches want to direct their players to college coaches they can trust.

AS YOU'RE ON THE ROAD RECRUITING YOUR ESTABLISHED PROSPECTS, ALWAYS TAKE A MOMENT TO ASK PREP COACHES WHO THE NEXT GREAT UP-AND-COMING PROSPECTS IN THE AREA ARE.

Yes, you will target heralded players who are getting lots of internet buzz and local publicity. But you can separate yourself as a recruiter by having great relationships and contacts everywhere that will give you early leads and insights on the next up-and-coming players that nobody has heard of yet! As you build your career, you want to be a recruiter who can identify talent early. The earlier you can identify talent, the earlier you can work to build relationships around the prospect and family, and the better your chances will be to sign great talent.

Another misconception that outsiders assume is that the really great coaches are only chasing 5-star talents, players at the top of every national Top 100 list. Wrong-- every great coach I've learned from has spent significant time recruiting unknowns who they'd only heard about through their trusted sources. At the end of the day, every great coach I've worked for never cared much about Top 100 rankings or internet buzz-- they only cared about prospects who they thought could make a difference for their team!

Having been within earshot of thousands of recruiting calls, I would hear college coaches ask prep coaches often, "Hey, so tell me who's a great player in your area that nobody's talking about."

As fans would rave about ranked players in our signing classes, I'd always think of the "unknowns" that our coaches were just as excited about. You can't base your evaluations off of internet buzz alone!

There are '8 Ways to Discover Players,' and you can use these channels to cast a wide net around your recruiting regions and within your position. As you're on the road recruiting your established prospects, always take a moment to ask prep coaches who the next great up-and-coming prospects in the area are. You need to build your lists for each graduating class in the next four years, not just the next year or two.

Yes, before you devote time, money and resources to go see specific players in person, you need to do your research. Unless the program turns out Division I after Division I prospect, do your homework to confirm measurables, watch video online and confirm skill before going out in person to evaluate a specific prospect.

8 WAYS TO DISCOVER PLAYERS

#1: National and Regional Scouting Services

#2: Regional or National Combines

#3: Tournaments and Games

#4: High School and AAU Coach Recommendations, particularly if the prep coach has had success throughout their career or has an established relationship with you

#5: Camps

#6: Highlight Videos

#7: Were Offered by a Rival or Comparable School

#8: Political Referrals: Boosters, alumni, former players, university employees, friend of top recruit, etc.

8 WAYS TO DISCOVER PLAYERS: SCOUTING SERVICES
#1: National and regional scouting services

One of the earliest and easiest ways to start building your "Watch List" will be though third-party scouting services. These subscription services generate reports for particular regions, events or even the ever-popular internet Top 100 lists. Particularly for underclassmen, these services help you cast a wide net and collect a lot of names – often broken down with recommendations for what level they will be recruited at.

There are independent scouts in most regions that put together lists for each grade within the state or region, and sell these lists to universities across the country. Most of these services include reports on each player's strengths and weaknesses (a few words to a few sentences), along with an estimated height and weight, school name and at times, contact information (email, phone number, home address).

As I tell recruits, just because a coach with a school-logoed polo isn't sitting in the stands, that doesn't mean that there isn't anyone there watching and taking notes. Coaches depend on these services to help start their research, especially for contact information and early evaluations they may provide on freshmen and sophomores!

Reports are generated from everywhere—Mississippi, Kansas, Georgia, Florida, New England, Texas, Illinois, Southern California, Northern California, Junior Colleges and on International players.

Many scouting reports will rate players as High Major+, High Major, High Major-, Mid-Major+, Mid-Major, Mid-Major-, Low-Major+, Low Major, Low Major-, Division II, Division III or NAIA. Or, Top FBS, Bottom FBS, Top FCS, Bottom FCS, DII, DIII or NAIA.

On a yearly basis, I've sat in recruiting meetings as our staff would go through Top 100 lists from popular internet sites and disagree with their rankings on many players. Oftentimes, one assistant coach would read off names and the other assistant coaches would respond with "overrated," "ehhhh," "a beast," "overrated," "slow," "good but not tough." Great coaches do their own complete evaluations and internet ranking plays zero influence on their thoughts of prospective student-athletes, don't necessarily buy into the internet hype as a young coach!

Staffs also cross-reference juniors and seniors on these regional reports to make sure that they haven't missed any late-bloomers or transplanted upperclassmen who have recently moved into the region. Again, the real value in these reports is often in finding the talented freshman and sophomores early or in building a complete list of potential players in the state, regionally or nationally.

These scouting service lists are just a starting point, a great early resource that can point you in the right direction!

8 WAYS TO DISCOVER PLAYERS: COMBINES
#2: *Impressive regional or national third-party combine results (height, weight, speed, testing results, notes)*

How do prospects stack up versus other players in the state, region or even nationally? Third-party combine results can be a great indicator of players with top physical measurements and for players who can produce great physical testing results.

Think of a smaller version of the NFL combine: if all players were put in a room, separated by position, measured up and put through the same drills, players will begin separating themselves from top to bottom, specifically with size, speed and testing measurements. Combine reports help you get an idea of more reliable measurements (likely verified or consistent).

A detailed report from each location (Orlando, Atlanta, Houston, Los Angeles, etc.) is sent to coaches across the country, including phone numbers, emails and mailing addresses for each combine participant. Each staff takes the data from each location and will add players to their Watch Lists accordingly based on their needs. Top measureables (height, weight, speed) are keys to add.

Size and speed can get prospects on your list, as position skills can be taught or improved.

8 WAYS TO DISCOVER PLAYERS: GAMES AND TOURNAMENTS
#3: Observed competing at a tournament or game

As you develop your "Watch Lists," they will drastically change throughout each recruiting cycle. You may add a prospect to your list based off combine results or scouting service recommendations but get out to see them play in person and not feel they're a fit, but add a teammate or player from the opponent team to your list. As you start following these leads and get out to scout prospects in person, you will undoubtedly find new additions that were previously unknown. And oftentimes, you will eliminate a good percentage of players that you initially came to see because of a lack of size, skill or attitude once you see them in person.

For example, you may take a list of 30 recommended prospects out to a tournament and add 10 additional players that you knew nothing about, while also eliminating 5-6 players after getting a chance to evaluate them in person.

You may travel out to a Friday night game to watch a prospect you've heard great things about, only to come back with 3-4 more names of players who stood out during the game. You have to always keep your eyes open, scouting for great size, speed, skill and players who just have "it."

Most staffs also cross-evaluate prospects, having multiple assistants evaluate them in person before offering a scholarship. Most head coaches also prefer to evaluate a player in person themselves before extending a scholarship offer, based off recommendations of multiple assistant coaches. Obviously, tremendous players are offered off of evaluations of one assistant coach and approved by the head coach, but most prospects are evaluated by multiple coaches before receiving an offer

While many prospects feel their only shot at getting discovered or recruited is if a college coach shows up at their school to watch a game, it's not the most common way to 'discover' players. First, as coaches, you need a REASON to go to the school to scout games for individual players. Unless the school or prep team churns out prospect after prospect each year, you need some great reasons to take time and resources to get to the competition site—don't just show up to a game unless you have a good reason!

What separates good prep players from great ones is how they perform versus other players in head-to-head competitions. Sounds like common sense—know that some players may look like the freshman superstar playing varsity on video but actually are unchallenged playing with and against weaker competition. How will they compete versus talented players in the area, how will they compete versus older and more physically developed players? Will they out-perform or will they be dominated versus great competition? Try to evaluation your prospects versus great competition.

Tournament events bring several players to one location, giving coaches a few days to see several or hundreds of prospects. Not all tournaments are created equal, find events that attract great competition and a quality level of talent (according to your program) when deciding which to scout.

NCAA rules change every year, usually with the intent to limit college coaches to very select evaluation periods. A common complaint coaches have is that these strict rules make it difficult for coaches to get enough good looks at a prospect in action, especially against quality competition. They may feel that it's not enough time in-person to gather complete information about several players that they are recruiting. Therefore, the system has evolved into third-party events that coaches can attend in person or receive results on.

When scouting events that attract several quality players, be sure to plan your schedule in advance and have all details prepared ahead of time. Who is playing where when? Schedule your time to maximize your coverage, along with scheduling time to support current commits if they are also competing.

YOU'LL NEED TO BALANCE YOUR TIME BETWEEN SUPPORTING FUTURE PLAYERS AND SCOUTING FOR NEW PROSPECTS.

When players commit to your program, that's not the end of your recruiting responsibilities. Some coaches spend a good amount of their time at these events just watching and supporting prospects who have already committed to their program, so you'll need to balance your time between supporting future players and scouting for new prospects.

During one evaluation period, I worked with a coaching staff that went to one city for two tournaments that had 996 combined games scheduled over a three-day period on 47 different courts across town. Each day, the first game started at 8am and the last game started at 9:45pm. Almost 1,000 games in three days on 47 courts around town, you can't imagine the planning and coordination that goes into outlining the most important games to get to and putting together a schedule to make sure that they were getting to see the maximum amount of prospects. Great coaches aren't just going to wander aimlessly at these events, they have a specific list of players to scout and a schedule to stick to. You may notice other players while scouting specific recruits, but you may not have time to wander aimlessly to find new players. You must have a plan before you get there!

Great players may have one or two bad games when you are in attendance. You may hesitate to cut them from your Watch List after one bad showing. On the same note, you want to make sure those one or two beastmode games that they had when you were in attendance weren't a fluke either. So the more you can see (or hear about) them competing versus other great players, or the more concrete research that you can get from trusted events, the better.

8 WAYS TO DISCOVER PLAYERS: RECOMMENDED BY PREP COACHES
#4: High school and AAU coach recommendations, particularly if the prep coach has had success throughout their career or has an established relationship with you

You will need to make daily recruiting calls to prep coaches, and this needs to be a habit you develop quickly. You will likely spend more time on the phone with prep coaches than you will with prospects, start building these relationships today! Within your recruiting regions, pick up the phone to say hello, get recommendations on top underclassmen, talk shop, check on their family/team, etc. You need to set a goal of how many prep coaches you need to reach out to daily, and use these sources to constantly build your "Watch Lists" for each graduating class. You need to develop the "Art of Conversation!"

As a staff, send out requests asking for recommendations and video of top freshmen, sophomores and juniors within your state and within the regions that you want to target.

Focus on a key region to build a "pipeline" in, and focus daily attention on growing your relationships in the area with ALL coaches, no matter if they have a prospect now or not.

Great recruiters are receptive when any prep coach calls. Prep coaches reach out to recommend a player or they may reach out about philosophy, drills or teaching tools. It's a good habit for college coaches to accept and return phone calls from any and every prep coach, and great recruiters will if they have the time. Down the road when they actually have a good prospect, prep coaches will remember you, you either treated them with respect or snubbed them.

WHEN MAKING YOUR CALLS AND VISITS, ALWAYS FOCUS ON THE FACT THAT YOU ARE BUILDING A CAREER. DON'T JUST CALL THE PREP COACHES WHO HAVE THE "HOT" PLAYERS NOW, YOU NEED TO REACH OUT TO AND BUILD RELATIONSHIPS WITH COACHES ACROSS EVERY LEVEL.

You can't spend too much time on the phone with everyone who calls you (see page 96) but at least give all prep coaches a quick call back as a sign of respect.

On the other hand, you will also run into prep coaches who won't offer any or much help. They may have allegiances to coaches at rival or competitor programs, be wrapped up in politics or are playing dirty -- so you need to learn to navigate around them and be prepared for some hesitation. There may be prep coaches who won't pass along your interest, mail, invitations or assist you with getting transcripts, grades or signatures. Every year I would run across a handful of players who didn't know our school was interested in them until later in the process because their high school or AAU coaches were unwilling to help provide us with their direct contact info or pass along mail. It's not uncommon for high school coaches to hide mail from select colleges because they have relationships with coaches at rival universities. Some prep coaches may request that all communication goes through them, not usually a great sign for your program.

A PREP COACH MAY NOT HAVE A GREAT RECRUITABLE PLAYER NOW, BUT THERE IS A GOOD CHANCE THAT YOU WILL RUN INTO THEM OVER THE NEXT FIVE, TEN, FIFTEEN YEARS.

For this reason, it's great to also have relationships with assistant coaches, coordinators, principals, guidance counselors and even secretaries, janitors and security guards. Sometimes you need to find other allies, other than the head coach.

Social media makes getting around this issue much easier than in past years, but remember you can only communicate with prospects directly if they are of age. You need to also work to find direct contact info (cell phones, email addresses, parents info) for prospects who play for prep coaches unwilling to assist. Prospects have the right to be aware of EVERY opportunity available to them, don't always take a prep coach's word for it if they tell you the prospect has no interest.

Each extra layer of "people" coaches must get through in order to get to the prospect is just another opportunity for the prospect to be taken advantage of, but it's a common situation for highly-rated prospects. You may have to call several people to finally get to the player, some prospects have huge circles around them.

Overcome the politics by building great contacts and relationships early in your career, they will be invaluable down the road! Even if you are at a small, unheard-of school now, realize that coworkers and prep coaches will be rising in the profession over the next 10-20 years. You never know where today's contacts will lead you, no matter where you are starting or where you currently are. Your recruiting career will depend on your relationships with prep coaches—period!

8 WAYS TO DISCOVER PLAYERS: CAMPS
#5: Stood out at a university camp

Throughout the year extend information on your summer camps to a wide range of prospects. Camps are important to most head coaches for a few reasons—as an opportunity to invite prospective players to campus and for additional income or staff bonuses.

Personally, I think camps are great for all prospects, even if they aren't a fit as a recruit for your program. They give athletes and high school students a great opportunity to get on a college campus, stay in the dorms for a few days, eat in the dining hall, see behind-the-scenes of the facility, meet other players who are also going through the same process. They may be disappointed that they don't make the cut for your program but the overall experience should be a motivating one for them, and a reality check of where they may fit in as a prospect.

Try to plan out your camp and clinic dates as early as possible each year so that you can share those dates with prospects and coaches while you are out on the road. Registration doesn't need to be open more than 3-4 months in advance, but having the details set gives you solid info to share with prospects. Have camp dates and details approved by the Athletic Department before you begin to publicize dates publically.

If sharing fields or courts with other teams, be sure to work out your camp dates with each other so there is no overlap. Don't try to slip by and call dibs on camp dates and facilities without working it out with the other teams that share your facilities or fields, this will only cause a firestorm and will likely end up with dates being canceled or moved. Eliminate confusion of having dates changed, and extra costs and time put into having brochures and websites redone. It's best in the long run to have everyone aware and signed off on camp dates before publicizing them.

With your priority recruits, emphasize your interest of getting them to campus for camp. Contact high school and AAU coaches immediately after dates are solidified and encourage them to bring their prospects or teams. As you are out visiting schools or speaking with prospects and coaches throughout the year, always pass along upcoming camp details. Carry brochures with you or even business cards with camp dates, websites, and phone numbers listed. As you are telling unsolicited prospects to send their video, tell them to consider your camp.

Recruit everyone for camp—year-round! Develop a system to collect email addresses or mailing addresses for camp brochures and e-blasts. Gather all the unsolicited emails and letters and put everyone's email address in an Excel file, and mailing address if you have the budget to send brochures out.

Camps can become cookie-cutter responsibilities to coaches, how can you separate your program to make your camps extremely memorable and enjoyable for ALL campers? What can you add from last year to make it more fun, a better learning experience or what other aspects of your program can you start including?

Most staffs host a variety of camps, ranging from all ages and skill levels to more "elite" camps. NCAA rules prohibit camps from being "invite only," all camps must be "open to any and all entrants, limited only by number, age, grade level and or gender." So any player who would like to attend (within this limitations) may do so. So as a staff you can organize camps that you may put more emphasis on inviting your top prospects, but you must not exclude anyone from signing up for reasons other than capacity. Speak to your Compliance Office on how you can organize such a camp, and the minimum amount of promotion you need to do.

NCAA rules also prohibit against recruiting during camps, coaches are not able to "extend verbal or written offers of financial aid to any prospective student-athlete during their attendance at a camp or clinic," give campus tours or set up meetings with faculty. BUT, camps are a good way for you to put a name with a face; to showcase your facilities; to introduce your coaching staff personally; to get a chance to see a prospects size, speed and skill in person; and for you to get to know the player and their family or mentor better.

If a camper is asking for an evaluation during camp, be tactful but don't sugarcoat the situation for them and lead them on. Compliment their strengths and give them a few pointers on areas they need to work on, extra credit if you want to show them a few drills they can work on once they get back home.

If you feel a player could make the cut at a friend's program-- pass along your business card and have them send video and a Student-Athlete resume (and a reminder of which school to forward it to) that you can share with a friend in the business.

CAMP TIPS:
- **REGISTRATION:** The day before check-in, get a list of campers who have registered. Are there any "Watch List" players who will be in attendance that you weren't expecting? Cross reference addresses, phone numbers, email addresses, parent info and other details with your database to see if you can fill in any blanks for your recruits.
- **TEAM CAMP:** Take time to recruit competitive regional teams or teams with recruits to your Team Camp, this will likely be a point of emphasis from your head coach. Team Camps often are more affordable for players and are great for helping build relationships with high school coaches, as well as helping them build team chemistry. Impress your head coach by getting a jump on securing quality, successful teams for Team Camp.
- **AFFORDABILITY:** Camps can be quite costly, especially if the prospect is attending them at multiple schools. Due to NCAA rules, you are unable to discount camp rates or offer need-based scholarships... but you are able to prorate fees on a day-by-day or practice-by-practice basis. For example, if a camp is $300 for 5 days, you can charge $60 for one day. By making camps more affordable, you can attract more prospects. All meals, t-shirts and instruction need to be paid for by all campers. Check with your Compliance Office on ways to minimize the cost issue.

- **ENERGY:** Don't sleepwalk through camps, help develop your position players for the short time that you have them. Share your favorite drills, tips and insight on what college coaches are look for at the position. Make sure your campers are having fun, most of them may be intimidated or nervous— encourage your campers, have fun and bring the energy to the huddle.

8 WAYS TO DISCOVER PLAYERS: HIGHLIGHT VIDEO
#6: Highlight videos

Again, the #1 rule that I tell prospects about getting discovered: For a coach to be interested in recruiting you, they must see you play first—either on video or in person. Since logistically it's expensive and time-consuming to get out on the road, collecting video is a great way to evaluate your potential prospects before investing time and money on travel.

Many third-party services gather film locally, regionally or nationally and sell packages and evaluations to coaches. Like scouting services, this is a good way to save some time and to collect some leads on names.

TO PREVENT PROSPECTS FROM SENDING MASS EMAILS TO EVERYONE ON STAFF, LIST EACH COACH'S RECRUITING REGIONS ON THE DIRECTORY.

Asking a prospect to send their video is a good way to put the ball back in their court. You will be approached by hundreds of players, parents and coaches each year telling you how talented they are, how passionate they are about your program, what a hard worker they are and how they just need a chance. Spending a lot of time on a prospect before you get a chance to see them compete for yourself (unless taking the early word of a very trusted source) is a waste of time. The best solution for these daily inquiries, "Sure, I'd love the chance to get to see them play, have them send over their video." Pass along your business card, a camp brochure, a smile and move on! Some will end up being recruits for you, many won't make the cut.

You need to spend time each day reviewing video— it's important that you have a system. Create a folder in your email to put unsolicited emails and links. Set time aside each day to watch prospect video.

WHEN CONTACTED OR APPROACHED BY UNKNOWN RECRUITS, A GOOD EARLY QUESTION TO ASK THEM IS, "TELL ME A LITTLE BIT ABOUT HOW RECRUITING IS GOING SO FAR? WHO HAVE YOU BEEN OFFERED BY OR HAVE YOU TAKEN ANY UNOFFICIAL VISITS?" IF THEY HAVE NO OFFERS, IT DOESN'T NECESSARILY MEAN THEY HAVE NO TALENT, JUST THAT THEY HAVEN'T BEEN DISCOVERED YET. FAST-TRACK YOUR IN-PERSON CONVERSATION TO GET A GAUGE OF HOW THEIR RECRUITING IS GOING SO FAR AND IF OTHER COACHES MAY HAVE ALREADY IDENTIFIED SOMETHING IN THEM.

RECRUITING MADE SIMPLE

VIDEO REVIEW:

- If the video is from a trusted source, or video you requested yourself, review in a timely manner.

- If the video was unsolicited and mailed or emailed to you, put it in a folder or pile to review as you get time. If from a competitive program, review it quickly.

- As a staff, sit down and watch video together of your top prospects. What feedback do the other assistant coaches provide and what are the head coach's thoughts? When making decisions on scholarship offers: the more sets of eyes, the better!

- If you immediately think they are a potential scholarship offer, show them to your head coach quickly for feedback. Offers for top prospects need to be made timely.

- Evaluate within the first few seconds if the prospect has the size and measureables to compete for your program. If they don't wow you within the first 30 seconds, move on.

- Once you have identified a prospect: Immediately add their basic mandatory information to the database (name, grad year, high school, a mailing address—home or school); send them a coded questionnaire (with your initials or marking to designate them as a prospect). When time allows, pick up the phone and call their prep coach; call your contacts in the area at rival schools; search for more information online; or if highly interested, and if the prospect is old enough, pick up the phone and call the prospect or their family immediately.

KEEP UNSOLICITED EMAILS/MAIL FROM PROSPECTS THROUGHOUT THE YEAR AND HAVE SUPPORT STAFF KEEP TRACK OF CONTACT INFORMATION FOR YOUR CAMP DATABASE. MAIL OR EMAIL YOUR CAMP BROCHURE OR WEBSITE TO EVERYONE ONCE REGISTRATION IS AVAILABLE.

Undoubtedly, it will be difficult to review and respond to everyone. If possible, have a system of responses as a staff. Forward all emails to a designated person who can mail/email questionnaires and camp brochures. This way, coaches aren't spending a lot of personal time on each unsolicited and underqualified prospect, but they are getting a response from your program. A small gesture goes a long way, even if it's a semi-rejection or next steps that need to be taken. It's a good practice to leave a good impression with everyone.

CUSTOMIZE THE ONLINE ATHLETIC DEPARTMENT STAFF DIRECTORY TO FIT YOUR PREFERENCES AS FAR AS LISTING YOUR DIRECT OFFICE NUMBER AND OFFICE EMAIL ADDRESS. SOME COACHES PREFER TO HAVE THEIR DIRECT INFORMATION LISTED, OTHERS PROVIDE ONE GENERIC TEAM PHONE NUMBER AND EMAIL ADDRESS AND FUNNEL IT INTERNALLY TO CUT DOWN ON UNSOLICITED EMAILS/CALLS GETTING DIRECTLY TO THE COACHES.

8 WAYS TO DISCOVER PLAYERS: RECRUITED BY A RIVAL
#7: Players offered by a rival or comparable school

Another common way to find potential prospects is to look into your rivals, conference members or comparable schools within the region – who are they offering? It is very common to hear a head coach go into an assistant coach's office and say, "Hey, the big kid from St. Louis just got offered by School XYZ, what did you think of them?" As an assistant coach, you need to know of EVERY potential prospect in your area or at your position, and have an answer of why you aren't recruiting them.

The internet is often buzzing about which prospects are receiving offers from which schools– scout your opponents off-the-field as well! You don't have to necessarily offer everyone they are offering but at least take an occasional look. Your head coach will be asking for your feedback of why rival prospects are not potential players for your program, make sure you've done your homework before asked.

8 WAYS TO DISCOVER PLAYERS: POLITICAL RECRUIT
#8: Political referrals (boosters, alumni, former players, university employees, friend of top prospect, etc.)

As you will be approached daily by prospects, parents and coaches bragging about the biggest talent you've never heard of, you will be pitched these prospects by some powerful people within the University and Athletic Department: long-time donors, University Board of Trustees members, former players, professional players, CEOs, celebrities. While it's ultimately the head coach's decision who is offered scholarships and who is not, part of your job is to always promote the program in a positive light and this includes giving some extra time to these people and following through with their leads, even if the players aren't talented enough for your program.

Or, one of your top prospects may be looking at schools with their best friend, wanting to play college sports together.

Many programs carry one or two players on their roster who are relatives of major boosters, donors or influential people within the University or Athletic Department, mostly as walk-ons. Your head coach may want to send mail and notecards to these type of players but may not be reserving a scholarship, rather simply saving them a spot as a priority walk-on.

Throughout my career I have worked with coaches who have actively recruited and offered players who were very talented, who just happened to be related to influential people or celebrities. Their connections may have nothing to do with why a player is recruited, it could 100% based on their talent.

But, business in any industry still revolves around this type of preferential treatment... that will never change. In the business of big money college athletics, these walk-on positions are sometimes given to those with influence around the program or University.

It's important to treat everyone with respect and put the ball back in their court. You don't necessarily have to devote time and recruiting resources (flights, days on the road, Official Visits) on these prospects early but definitely place a return phone call, mail a questionnaire and send a camp brochure.

Speak with the head coach about how they would like to handle each situation, every political relationship is different. Take the lead of your head coach. Would they want to hold a priority walk-on position for them, do they want you to initiate a campus visit or phone call?

CHAPTER #2
GATHERING INFO

"Sports don't build character; they reveal it."
-HEYWOOD HALE BROUN

"Don't make them in your image. Don't even try. My assistants don't look alike, think alike, or have the same personalities. And I sure don't want them thinking the way I do. You don't strive for sameness; you strive for balance."
-BEAR BRYANT

"If your focus is on what you can put into people rather than what you can get out of them, they'll love and respect you."
-JOHN C. MAXWELL

"Three things cannot be long hidden: the sun, the moon, & the truth."
-BUDDAH

GATHERING INFO: IMPORTANCE OF GREAT DATA

Once you have identified potential prospects you want to recruit, selling them your program depends on two things:

#1 - Gathering accurate contact info
#2 - Putting together top selling points about your program individually tailored to them

In order to get your prospects to campus for a visit and to get serious consideration, you will need to draw them in and show them how your program is a "great fit," full of opportunities. Getting prospects to visit you is vital, especially early in the process. In order to get prospects interested in visiting, you must be extremely organized in these two areas: gathering accurate contact info and developing great "selling points."

Programs are evaluating and actively recruiting hundreds of prospects, so an organized system is crucial. It's impossible to remember everything on your own or dig through notes scratched on post-it pads or in notebooks, and you don't want to spend all of your time tracking down individual phone numbers and email addresses on an as-needed basis.

> IF YOU DON'T HAVE THE PLAYER'S HOME ADDRESS, SEND QUESTIONNAIRES AND MAIL TO THE HIGH SCHOOL. SOME PLAYERS PREFER TO HAVE MAIL SENT TO THE HIGH SCHOOL, ASK YOUR TOP PLAYERS IF THEY HAVE A PREFERENCE OF WHERE'D THEY LIKE TO RECEIVE MAIL. IF THEY'RE ALREADY ON YOUR MAILING LIST, ASK THEM IF THEY'RE RECEIVING IT.

As you add prospects to your "Watch List," immediately, put their **name, graduation year, high school and internal ranking code** into the database, those four fields are mandatory. Immediately after they're entered into the system, drop a questionnaire in the mail. It's important that when you send a questionnaire to a priority recruit that you also immediately add them to the database in the meantime with the mandatory details, and work on getting the other contact info blanks filled in through several sources.

You can have a great opportunity for your prospects but if you don't have correct phone numbers, addresses, email addresses and social media accounts-- your messages won't be heard. As a staff, you need to cast a wide net with underclassmen, and collect as much contact info that you can—early! Good databases take time to build, you need to start gathering contact information months or years before you can legally contact players. Start sending out your legal mailings—questionnaires and camp brochures-- early to freshmen and sophomores while the process is still new and exciting to them.

Have a member of your support staff take responsibility and pride in building a quality contact database. This information needs to be accessible to you and your staff instantaneously—on paper, on your phone, through an app. You need to be able to access phone numbers 24/7 of all prospects that you are allowed to contact, their coaches and their parents.

WHEN YOU DISCOVER A PRIORITY RECRUIT YOU: IMMEDIATELY ADD CRITICAL DATA (NAME, GRAD YEAR, HIGH SCHOOL, YOUR INTERNAL RANKING) + SEND A QUESTIONNAIRE THAT DAY!

GATHERING INFO: ORGANIZED ACROSS THE BOARD

One of the biggest difference-makers in recruiting is organization as a staff, you can quickly get overwhelmed and running in 50 different directions without a system. Organization and consistency will help you get through stressful times, your day-by-day job is unpredictable, so being organized and prepared for anything that you can takes the pressure off you for the unplanned chaos that comes up!

It is important that you are professional with everyone you work with- prospects, parents, coaches, internal support staff, university staff, vendors—and one of the biggest aspects of being professional is being organized. Strive to prepare for each event with every perspective in mind. You should be at a point where you are organized enough to be looking a month ahead (or more) for every event you manage.

ORGANIZE WEEKLY OR MONTHLY RECRUITING PLANNING MEETINGS TO ANTICIPATE UPCOMING EVENTS AND DEADLINES. PLAN AHEAD EVERY DETAIL THAT YOU CAN, AND GIVE AS MUCH NOTICE THAT YOU CAN TO THE GROUPS YOU WORK WITH.

Key data (cell phone numbers and email addresses) need to be easily accessible for all prospects, parents and high school coaches 24/7! You need to have immediate access to this information at a moment's notice as your head coach will come into your office and want to jump on a call now – be prepared!

- **ASSISTANT COACH SUPPORT:** For coaches to do their job efficiently, a support staff that can help streamline, organize, prepare and manage non-coaching details is essential. A great head coach has assistant coaches who are prepared, and to put assistant coaches in a great position, you need a great support staff, grad assistants, interns, managers and gameday volunteers. In-season operations, evaluation periods, camps and Official/Unofficial Visit events are of utmost importance to coaches, therefore it's a game changer to have a strong support staff that can streamline procedures. The goal of your support staff is to handle responsibilities that can be taken off the plates of assistant coaches, freeing them up to make more phone calls, visits or to spend more time on gameplans, relationships with players and practice preparations.

- **DATABASE:** The prospect and prep coaches databases need to be proofed continuously with limited access granted to select staff. It is important that information is pooled for everyone's use and that it is correct- prospect names, addresses, phone numbers, coach's info. When too many people have hands in editing the database, it can be tough to manage. In most cases, it's better to only have a couple people update new addresses, phone numbers, etc.

When making updates to the database, keep the handwritten notes of addresses or phone numbers in a drawer or file. Typos are common, store those original copies somewhere in case you need to look back on them!

When gathering prospect information you may run across multiple spellings of first and last names, ask their head coach or ask the prospect directly. Have a point person in charge of confirming the correct spellings of your prospects names and prep coaches, via the internet and social media, or by making phone calls if unsure. Misspellings are insulting!

- **ACADEMICS:** Admissions information, as well as specific college and major booklets, needs to be on hand, as well as contacts established within each department. As recruiters, you need to show that you know as much about academics as you do your sport. All university admittance and academic policies need to be understood and easily recited. Every coach needs to understand University GPA and test score standards without having to look them up.

- **ATHLETIC DEPARTMENT AND UNIVERSITY CONTACTS:** Communication is key between your team's support staff and contacts within the Athletic Department and the University. You are working with other departments and non-athletics staff at times, give them as much preparation time and advanced notice that you can, and remember to be appreciative of their assistance. Don't expect them to drop everything they're doing to help you, especially consistently.

- **EVENTS:** Events need to be thoroughly planned out to eliminate as many kinks as possible. Every procedure needs to be simplified and smooth, recruiting events will be held year-round, so you need to develop a streamlined system. Constantly evaluate ways to simplify your procedures. Ask the external groups that you work with for input on ways to improve.

Set dates early for Junior/Sophomore Days, group Unofficial Visit weekends, Official Visit weekends, camps and clinics. When you pick dates early, you can begin setting up all the operational details and begin inviting players, coaches and parents.

Have an operations coordinator manage event logistics or assign individual responsibilities among the coaching staff for housing, meals, venue reservations, security, Compliance approvals, gear, check-in, payment processes, staffing schedules, intern assistance, etc.

- **CALENDAR:** Put together a detailed calendar that is complete with important high school and University dates, and dates important within your season, conference, and sport. Be looking a month ahead and find ways that you can connect with all of your audiences: pre-season, conference season, post-season, first day of class, final exams, Prom, Super Bowl, NFL combine, AAU tourneys, graduation, holidays. Know what is coming up in the next few weeks!

Sit down with your Compliance Office to be aware of all paperwork you must submit regarding evaluations, recruiting travel, phone logs, visitors on campus to make paperwork easier to complete. Keep a very detailed calendar listing evaluations, traveling, phone calls.

- **EVALUATION DAYS:** The NCAA limits coaches to a certain number of in-person evaluations, limits vary by sport. A central person needs to maintain these logs of dates, locations, prospects seen and coaches from your staff in attendance. You may have to plan out your evaluations to not exceed these limits, as well as the total number of days on the road recruiting. Organization is essential for keeping track of evaluation days.

It's time-consuming to have to go back and research your moves from weeks or months ago. Develop a system or file to track all necessary Compliance information as you go.

> **ONE OF THE MOST NON-COACHING TIME-WASTERS IS GETTING MIXED UP IN BUSINESS OFFICE AND COMPLIANCE PAPERWORK AND CHALLENGING REIMBURSEMENT REJECTIONS. DON'T LET THESE EVERY DAY PROCEDURES TAKE AWAY FROM YOUR CORE RESPONSIBILITIES!**

- **BUSINESS OFFICE:** Get to know reimbursement policies and spending allowances/per diems ahead of time. All schools vary with their travel policies for hotels, flights and meals. Develop a system to keep all receipts, hotel bills, flight reservations, meals, tolls, mileage, etc. You can quickly run up thousands of dollars in bills and some universities are quite picky about reimbursement policies and spending allowances. You don't want to end up paying for expenses personally—which can happen if you don't follow University policy! Ask other coaches in the Athletic Department how long it takes for reimbursements to be processed, and if there are other landmines to look out for.

- **CORRESPONDENCE:** A flowchart of communication needs to be developed for solicited and unsolicited correspondence (calls, mail, email, DVDs) so each inquiry will receive a response from your program, either via mail or email.

- **CORRECT SPELLING:** Spell names correctly! Between the internet, combine reports, AAU packets... even the simplest names can have multiple spellings from your reports. When gathering info, be sure to ask prep coaches for correct name spellings for players, parents and coaches. Although it may seem like a minor detail, an easy error to mistake a y for an i, for a typo to happen when entering hundreds of prospects into the database. As you scoff when you are wrongly addressed or your name is mispronounced, understand kids and parents do too! Take the extra time to make sure your prospects' names are spelled correctly!

- **TRANSCRIPTS:** Keep a file cabinet or binder for all transcripts gathered, either by staff or for yourself. Create a file for each prospect in a central location or organize on your own in alphabetical order. Transcripts are needed for Official Visits and a variety of reasons, depending on the campus. Be sure that transcripts are immediately returned to the cabinet after use, or that you make a copy before giving to someone on staff to review.

FOCUS ON TODAY'S DETAILS, BUT ALWAYS BE PLANNING FOR THE NEXT FEW MONTHS. WHAT EVENTS AND MILESTONES ARE COMING UP?

GATHERING INFO: KEEP EVERYTHING

As you are building your "Watch Lists" and gathering hundreds of phone numbers, emails, family contacts and prep coach cells, it's always important to keep a hard copy on file of all your hard-earned data.

Databases and hard drives crash, or you may be fired or move on and take another job. Having worked through several coaching changes—some quite unexpected—most universities quickly shut down access to computers, emails, and phones—often disabled immediately or moments prior to firing!

It's also good practice to keep your handwritten notes with phone numbers, emails and addresses for a bit—typos are common in large databases and having the original notes can be a big time-saver for you if you realize the phone number listed in the database is wrong. Keep a rolling notebook available when making calls or keep a pile of sticky notes in a drawer so you can always go back and find the correct contact info.

For whatever reason, you don't want to be left empty-handed so it's good practice to weekly or monthly print out your prospect/prep coach lists and keep a copy. Make this a weekly habit!

GATHERING INFO: DISTANCE FROM HOME

One of the early conversations that you need to have with your top prospects is the 'distance from home' factor. Distance from home is one of the most common factors that can eliminate you or help you.

Over the years, I've seen parents literally threaten to disown their kids if they decided to move across the country to attend our school, a player leave pre-season camp and walk home on the interstate (and he only lived and hour and a half from campus), players choose to go elsewhere to get away from family or players transfer to be closer to their girlfriends or moms.

Some players specifically want to stay close to home, where plenty of friends and family can come see them play regularly. If you are recruiting a player long-distance who is very family-oriented, it may be tough to get them to actually make the decision to leave. They may look around, take visits, try to keep an open mind... but no matter what the playing situation may be, they just may never be able to leave.

On the same note, other players are on the first flight out-of-town after graduation. They can't wait to get out of their little town or away from the big city and make a lifestyle change. Some players have absolutely no issues moving far away from home, being further than a car ride away from family. The athletic and academic situation may heavily outweigh any issues about leaving home. Some players may be running from family situations, parenthood or boredom or just running to a different type of life.

Some schools are in a city that is naturally a big draw: New York, Los Angeles, Miami.... nationally, these schools are able to generate excitement based off the fact that they're in exciting global cities. On the other hand, these schools face a lot of negativity from parents. Every community has its strengths and weaknesses, and these vary by family.

In the end, a lot of final decisions come down to the distance factor, and a lot of transfers are related to distance from home. Take time with each prospect to have this conversation early, before you get too deep in the process. Not that you shouldn't recruit a player that may be indecisive about leaving home, just always remember this could be an issue down the road and evaluate how hard you will pursue them with your resources.

If your location has resulted in a lot of interest but lack of commitments from your top prospects, evaluate the type of players you are recruiting and what regions they're from. You may need to focus more general attention on players from cities similar to yours so they won't be scared away.

GATHERING INFO: QUESTIONAIRES

NCAA rules prohibit sending mail to most athletes until some time during their junior year--with the exception of camp brochures and questionnaires—so make the most of these opportunities!

Save time by having a stack of envelopes stuffed with questionnaires ready to be sent out—they're just waiting to have a name and address slapped on them and dropped in the mail. Be sure to include a postage-paid, pre-addressed return envelope that's already addressed back to your program.

You can also save time by coding questionnaires before they're sent out with a tiny colored dot or recruiting coaches' initials written in the corner. If it's a high-priority recruit, possibly a green dot in the top corner and if it's a low-priority recruit, a red dot in the same spot so that when they are returned, the high priority ones can be photocopied and given to the recruiting coach and immediately entered into the database to receive mail and emails. You can also write your name on the pre-addressed envelope to help direct the questionnaire to your mailbox before getting sorted into other hands.

Giving out questionnaires can be a gesture of good will, a move that is cheap and quick. Prep coaches will call and recommend a player that you may have no interest in, prospects and their parents may drop by the office unannounced, a University booster may reach out to you about a lead... these are all instances where you can easily and quickly wrap up a conversation by handing them a questionnaire and put the ball back in their court. Give them a pre-coded questionnaire as a low-priority prospect to save time, ask them to send their video or consider attending a camp and move on!

If you have the administrative staff, it never hurts to keep up with the low-priority recruits in the database or keep them filled alphabetically by class for future reference. Guaranteed, some of these players who come to you first will improve in a year or two and can eventually be great prospects for you—and boom, you may already have all their vital information gathered and entered in the database.

HAVE PRE-STUFFED ENVELOPES READY WITH QUESTIONNAIRES AND POSTAGE-PAID RETURN ENVELOPES ENCLOSED SO THAT YOU CAN EASILY PUT A NAME AND ADDRESS ON THE ENVELOPE AND DROP IN THE MAILBOX IMMEDIATELY!

CODE QUESTIONNAIRES TO SEPARATE THEM FROM LEGITIMATE RECRUITS AND ONES YOU ARE SENDING OUT TO BE POLITE. PUT YOUR INITIALS OR LAST NAME ON THE OUTSIDE OF THE POSTAGE-PAID RETURN ENVELOPE TO HAVE PRIORITY RECRUIT QUESTIONNAIRES RETURNED DIRECTLY TO YOU.

BY SENDING A QUESTIONNAIRE IMMEDIATELY AFTER YOU ADD A PROSPECT TO YOUR "WATCH LIST" IN THE DATABASE YOU INCREASE YOUR CHANCES OF BEING ONE OF THE FIRST SCHOOLS TO SHOW INTEREST, OR SHOW A SENSE OF URGENCY AFTER TALKING TO THEIR PREP COACH. SEND QUESTIONNAIRES OUT QUICKLY!

Especially within the state or region, and among freshman and sophomores, distribute questionnaires freely. By focusing on building a strong database of contacts early-- players (and parents) are more likely to return them early before the recruiting process becomes overwhelming and time-consuming. By the time they are juniors, they're less likely to return them.

By sending questionnaires early you're also making a good first impression by being one of the first coaches or programs to express interest. Being one of the first schools to show interest is an ego-booster, and sometimes builds a little extra loyalty into a players' psychology.

GATHERING INFO: NICKNAMES OR PREFERRED NAMES
Always ask the prospect when name or nickname they prefer to go by. Always refer to them and address mail to their preferred name or nickname. Save their real names for Compliance paperwork.

GATHERING INFO: SCOUTING REPORTS / AAU PACKETS
Scouting service reports, AAU tournament packets and combine results are great resources for building your prospect databases! As you collect these recommendations and testing reports, hang on to them for updates to the database. Many reports list high schools, grad year, prep coach info (name, cell, email), prospect info (mailing address, cell phone numbers, email address), along with physical data (guestimates or confirmed data), all valuable information!

Highlight players to add to your Watch List or players currently on your Watch Lists and have support staff add to or update your prospect database. Oftentimes cell phone numbers change, addresses change or prospects transfer to other high schools so it's always good practice to check current info. When adding or changing cells, addresses or emails it's also a good practice to keep the previous info somewhere- don't delete phone numbers entirely, but make a note of which is the new number.

WHEN ADDING OR CHANGING CELLS, ADDRESSES OR EMAILS IT'S ALSO A GOOD PRACTICE TO KEEP THE PREVIOUS INFO SOMEWHERE- DON'T DELETE PHONE NUMBERS ENTIRELY, BUT MAKE A NOTE OF WHICH IS THE NEW NUMBER.

GATHERING INFO: PHONE CALLS
Over the year your staff will get plenty of unsolicited calls. Take the time to train administrative staff to screen callers to filter prospects. While many of your recruits have your direct cell phone numbers, you'd be surprised by the number of quality prospects who call the main office number on their own.

- Screen callers and gather the basic information:
    - Name
    - Grade
    - High School
    - City
    - Position
    - Phone Number
    - Email Address
    - Mailing Address
- Put the caller on hold and check to see if the prospect is in the database.
    - If the prospect is in the database and highly rated, let them know exactly which coach is their recruiting coach and ask if they would like their direct office number before transferring. If a top prospect, try to make immediate contact with the coach to take the call on the spot.
    - If the prospect is not in the database, tell them to send their video in the meantime and that you'll pass their information along but:
        - "The coaches are in a staff meeting."
        - "The coaches are in a team meeting."
        - "The coaches are out of town recruiting."
        - "The coaches are at lunch."
        - "Coach is in an interview now with the media."
    - Take a moment to Google the player or look up in video databases to see if anything comes up that can help you get a better understanding of the player's abilities.

GATHERING INFO: SOCIAL MEDIA
Once your recruits are old enough to contact legally, hitting them up on social media is one of the quickest ways to start gathering more accurate contact info.

Print your "Watch List" and search for each prospect on Facebook, Twitter, Instagram, Snapchat, Periscope or whatever platform is hot right now. Try to confirm that it's correct profile, double-checking the high school or hometown, if listed. You can also check their pictures (if visible) and confirm if athletic pictures are in the correct jersey of their prep team.

BE SURE THAT YOUR SOCIAL MEDIA ACCOUNTS CLEARLY SHOW WHAT SCHOOL YOU WORK FOR! SPELL IT OUT, NOT ALL ABREVIATIONS OR LOGOS ARE KNOWN BE PROSPECTS. INCLUDE A LINK TO YOUR PROGRAM'S PAGE.

IT'S IMPORTANT TO REMEMBER, DUE TO NCAA RULES YOU MAY NOT COMMUNICATE WITH THEM PUBLICALLY, EVERYTHING MUST BE DONE BY DIRECT OR PRIVATE MESSAGE. IF YOU ARE NEW TO SOCIAL MEDIA HAVE A GRAD ASSISTANT GIVE YOU A CRASH COURSE AND STAY CURRENT ON NCAA RULES OF SOCIAL MEDIA DO'S AND DON'TS—ASK YOUR COMPLIANCE OFFICE FOR SPECIFIC CURRENT SOCIAL MEDIA RULES.

As long as they're old enough per NCAA rules, add them and message them for their cell phone number, email address and mailing address. You don't want to overwhelm them with long messages for too much information but at least ask for their cell phone number, email or mailing address. You can also include a link to your online questionnaire for them to fill out and send them your direct cell phone number and tell them to contact you at any time.

Post pictures to look more authentic—your position group, behind scenes pictures and family pictures are all great to share!

You can also learn a lot about your prospects through their social media posts and get an even better feel about their personality, circle of friends and likes or dislikes. You might actually be shocked of what you can learn about your prospects, including:

- Athletic or Academic Honors and Awards
- Drug use
- Constant use of vulgar language
- Visiting rival campuses
- On campus at other schools you've never discussed
- Camping at other schools
- Family on campus at other schools
- Decommitting via social media
- Committing via social media
- Arrests
- They've become a parent
- They got engaged or married
- More about their personalities, hobbies, likes and dislikes
- Who their boyfriend/girlfriend is
- The circle of friends they keep

You may not be getting the whole story from conversations with your prospects! Social media can help you get to know your prospects personalities, hobbies, likes and dislikes and may tell you more than you'd like to know!

*"COACHES HAVE TO
WATCH FOR WHAT THEY DON'T WANT TO SEE
AND LISTEN TO WHAT THEY DON'T WANT TO HEAR."
–JOHN MADDEN*

GATHERING INFO: HIGH SCHOOL COACH DATABASE

Assign a staffer to manage the high school coach database, it's critical that names are filled in (mail not addressed to 'Head Coach') and that names are spelled correctly.

When mail is returned have support staff to make a habit of following up to see why. Is the head coach no longer there, has the school moved?

Annually, check to confirm that the head coach is still in place, or update with the new coaches' information. Get new cells and email addresses of new coaches as the new school year starts.

If you have the resources and manpower, you can expand your coach database to include assistant coaches at prep programs. If possible, include them in mailouts or e-blasts. This group also may have influence on prospects and may aspire to be head coach's themselves, it doesn't take much extra effort to build an early relationship starting with e-blasts.

If hosting coaching clinics, get email addresses of all attendees to include in your e-blasts. Share philosophy, drills, team chemistry exercises, motivational quotes and good luck or congratulations with them!

GATHERING INFO: STAY UPDATED ON PROSPECT NEWS

A quick way to stay updated on the progress of your top prospects: create a Google Alert to have up-to-date information and news articles sent directly to your inbox for FREE!

TO SIGN UP FOR GOOGLE ALERTS:
- Log into www.Google.com/alert
- Under 'Search Query' type in the prospect's name. If a common name, type in their name and high school (example: John Thompson Westlake)
- Under 'How Often' select the frequency you'd like to receive updates
- Under 'Your Email' enter the email address you would like alerts to go to
- Hit 'Create Alert' button
- Repeat again for each prospect that you would like to receive alerts on
- Check your email address to confirm that you would like to receive the alerts for each individual player. You must confirm each one separately.

CHAPTER #3
EVALUATIONS

"How you select people is more important than how you manage them once they're on the job. If you start with the right people, you won't have problems later on."
-JOHN C. MAXWELL

"The main ingredient of stardom is the rest of the team."
-JOHN WOODEN

"Success demands singleness of purpose."
-VINCE LOMBARDI

"Great leaders are not defined by the absence of weakness, but rather by the presence of clear strengths."
-JOHN ZENGER

EVALUATIONS: RESPONSIBILITIES AS A STAFF

Nearly every program splits recruiting responsibilities between the staff, primarily by geographic region, position or grade. Each staff may designate an assistant coach as the coordinator but each assistant coach has an equal responsibility to sign players. One of the first assignments as a staff is to delegate these responsibilities effectively. Which coach will be responsible for which group of prospects? Will you cross-recruit and assign multiple coaches to top prospects?

For example, will each assistant coach be responsible for specific geographic regions – and also expected to be involved in recruiting players at their position?

Head coaches are very involved in the recruiting process but most only get involved with players who have already been identified as great prospects for the program. Head coaches aren't gathering video, making initial evaluations and calling prep coaches to find the next up-and-coming prospects. As prep players approach head coaches, they will likely refer them down to the recruiting coordinator or appropriate assistant coach to do the appropriate research, after a cordial hello.

How will you be organized as a staff to attack your key areas effectively?

The home state is often divided into small regions, giving each assistant coach an assigned area to monitor and build relationships in. Most college programs make it a priority to keep the best players in the state at home, making sure that each of the assistant coaches play a role in identifying ALL potential recruits in the state. Each assistant is often assigned a handful of counties within the state to become an expert in.

> **IT'S A GOOD PHILOSOPHY TO PUT ATTENTION INTO EVERY IN-STATE PREP PROGRAM, EVEN IF THEY CURRENTLY HAVE NO PROSPECTS. YOU ARE BUILDING LONG-TERM RELATIONSHIPS FOR THE FUTURE, BOTH FOR YOUR PROGRAM AND FOR YOUR PERSONAL CAREER.**

Major regional and national metropolitan areas are assigned after that, depending on the radius that your head coach wants to recruit. Major cities have more affordable and accessible flights, so head coach's will put an emphasis on recruiting major cities and outlying towns. For example, coaches are normally assigned (depending on the region) to cities like Atlanta, DC/Baltimore, Miami, Dallas, Houston, Tampa, Chicago, Los Angeles, Minneapolis and Kansas City. Key states and regions are assigned from there— Florida, California, Texas, Northeast, Midwest, West Coast and so on, depending on your sport. Staffs cover the map— including assigning International and Junior College contacts.

Depending on your program's reach, the head coach may not have a preference about signing in-state players versus out-of-state players—only concerned with the best signing class possible. You never want to lose a top player in the state to an out-of-state school, so it's important to make a great impression within the state.

Most major programs will recruit nationally for the best talent possible, but still often paying attention in a few areas where they have had success. Smaller schools may focus regionally since they have smaller budgets, preferring to make a name for themselves locally instead. For smaller schools, it's better to focus on prospects within driving distance instead of constantly flying coaches across the country, or regularly flying recruits in on expensive flights. Each school has a regional focus on recruiting, but vary with the level of emphasis that they put on recruiting on a national level, usually dependent on their budget or historical success at home.

PUT TOGETHER A LIST OF ALL HOME-STATE COUNTIES WITH RECRUITING COACH ASSIGNMENTS. BEYOND THAT, LIST REGIONAL AND NATIONAL ASSIGNMENTS. HAVE BOTH A COLOR-CODED MAP AND A COUNTY-BY-COUNTY LIST SHOWING ASSISTANT COACH COVERAGE (WITH HIGH SCHOOL ASSIGNMENTS) AND SHARE WITH ADMINISTRATIVE AND RECRUITING ASSISTANTS WHO ANSWER THE PHONE AND GENERIC EMAILS. HAVE ALL PROSPECTS DIRECTED TO THE APPROPRIATE ASSISTANT COACH TO BEGIN CONVERSATIONS.

Always work with long-term goals in mind, so that once the school or coach HAS a great player you will already have close relationships with the coaching staff. You're never just building for the current season, you're building for your entire career! Your long-term relationships in key recruiting areas are extremely important career-wise, building strong ties in these regions can help you get and keep jobs in the future.

Head coaches will assign geographic responsibilities to assistants based on the previous ties of each coach. For example, when an SEC head coach hires their assistants, they all need strong Southern ties, locking down Georgia, Florida, Alabama, Mississippi and the Carolinas. They will also need a mix of coaches with ties to the Northeast, East Coast, Midwest, Texas and West Coast. Same for West Coast teams, they have assistant coaches with ties across California, Washington and Oregon as well as a mix of staff that has strong ties to the Midwest, Northeast and the South.

Assistant coaches are assigned specific geographic regions because they're an

YOUR LONG-TERM RELATIONSHIPS IN RECRUITING REGIONS ARE EXTREMELY IMPORTANT TO YOUR CAREER! RELATIONSHIPS WITH PREP COACHES AND PREP PROGRAMS IN HOTBED REGIONS CAN HELP YOU GET AND KEEP JOBS!

area they grew up in, went to college in, have worked in before or have previous ties to. It's helpful for coaches to have personal ties to regions: parents of recruits (and their extended families) oftentimes have mutual friends with college coaches, which helps in building relationships during the process. It always helps if a coach is a friend of a cousin, brother, mother and those ties can go back decades. You will want parents and recruits to feel a built-in familiarity, and that has a lot to do with long-term personal relationships. Good or bad, you will have a 'track record' in your previous regions.

When cross-recruiting by region and position, have a "primary recruiter" listed who will be responsible for tracking allowable calls, visits and evaluations. They take the lead as organization and communication is critical about calls and visits. Since contacts and evaluations are limited within most sports, one coach needs to be the primary recruiter responsible for tracking these.

EVALUATIONS: BUILDING YOUR 'WATCH LIST' OF PROSPECTS

Organization on a high level is critical to becoming a great recruiter. While relationships will be your biggest strength, organization is also critical!

You need to work off an ever-changing list of players that you've identified, let's call it your 'Watch List.' You will constantly be adding and subtracting names from your personal list. As a staff, begin to build a master list for each graduating class, building lists for several classes in advance. Just because you can't contact prospects as freshmen or sophomores, that doesn't mean that you shouldn't be getting organized and doing your research on underclassmen.

Since there is so much information to gather and keep track of on thousands of prospects, coaches and parents — an organized system is essential, for both you personally and as a staff.

You can save valuable hours by having contact information correct and accessible at your fingertips – you don't want to waste minutes and hours tracking down correct cell phone numbers and office numbers. When your head coach walks into your office and wants to get so-and-so on the phone right now, they mean right now, not in a few hours. You can't constantly work off a list of names and numbers scribbled in notebooks or Google every contact along the way.

Every school has a recruiting database— some cost thousands of dollars while others are simple Excel files. Within major programs, databases are updated daily, with players constantly being added and internal rankings changing! Many databases have email features and are able to keep track of more information than you'd ever want to know about. Are all the bells and whistles nice? Sure— but ultimately they're not all necessary. Having quality, correct info is more important. You can still get results with an Excel file and a Constant Contact email account.

In the first chapter we reviewed the eight ways to start collecting prospect leads, prospects to be added to your Watch List. Once you add names to your database you will need to rank them internally, based on how much attention they need to receive. If prospects aren't ranked internally, they disappear into a black hole! Your Watch List needs to be printed out and with you daily, accessible on paper, by phone and online. You always want to have your recent updates saved on paper and digitally, as well.

There will be a scramble in the time from when you add prospects to your Watch List... to getting a chance to personally evaluate them for yourself... to getting a feel for their intangibles, their raw athletic talent and their interest level in your program. Your Watch List of juniors and seniors will change weekly or daily!

You need to constantly be adding quality freshmen and sophomores to your database based off observations from games, practices and tournaments as well as from reports produced by regional scouting services that you subscribe to. If you see someone you like, even if they're too young, add them to the database for future reference!

You are building this list, sending questionnaires and gathering contact information so that you will be prepared to contact them once you are legally able to, according to NCAA rules. It's best to begin collecting contact information early!

The best recruiters are always three steps ahead in their research and evaluations, and they're always trying to discover the best players in the area before every other college does, and building those relationships with prep coaches and high schools early.

These Watch Lists are a great point of reference to use when planning your recruiting travel schedules to evaluate prospects. Coaches take their base Watch List out on the road at the beginning of each evaluation period and will add and subtract recruits based on in-person evaluations. Your Watch List will be very fluid, especially early in each recruiting cycle until you can begin to evaluate players in person.

For example, you may have a list of 25-30 top "A" players that you have gathered leads on from trusted sources and are still trying to evaluate another 20 potential "B" players. After those in-person evaluation periods on the road, you will likely drop five to ten "A" players but come back with 10 new names to add, including bumping up some "B" players to "A." These lists are just a first reference point before evaluations.

Even if you add a prospect to your Watch List because they are on a national or state Top 100 lists, that doesn't mean that you will think they are a good fit for your system and program. And just because a prospect isn't on any Top 100 lists, it doesn't mean that they can't help you win. Great recruiters can sense talent pretty quickly and it doesn't matter if they are a 5-star player or an unranked player. If you like their skills—and you think they can help you win– add them to your list. Trust your gut!

It's better to have a list that's too big than to have one that is too small, especially for the underclassmen.

*ORGANIZE YOURSELF IN YOUR OWN WAY,
NO COACH DOES IT THE SAME WAY.
WHAT WORKS BEST FOR YOU IN TERMS OF COLLECTING AND
ORGANIZING INFORMATION IS WHAT WORKS BEST, PERIOD!*

EVALUATIONS: TRANSFERS & JUCO PLAYERS

Many staffs put some level of attention into evaluating and recruiting Junior Colleges. Other programs consider transfer students, depending on the strength of their depth chart and upperclassmen. If your upcoming roster is pretty young, consider signing a few JuCo's or transfers for key positions that lack depth.

Junior College athletes were often good high school prospects who had academic or personal issues that disrupted or ended their college recruiting. They may have attended a JuCo to improve their test scores or grades, to stay close to home or to focus on growing athletically. Some JuCo players are late bloomers who are re-doing the recruiting process.

For whatever reason, JuCo transfers can provide an immediate boost of physical maturity, age and sometimes maturity to your roster. Junior College players have already been through their first round of being away from home and the responsibilities that come with that.

Second chances are not only for players, but for coaches as well. You may get turned down during the recruiting process only for a player to pick up the phone in a year or two and express their interest in transferring to your program. Always try to leave a recruiting relationship on good terms when your top prospects sign with other programs, you never know, they may come play for you one day after all!

Recruits are pulled in several directions during the process and although they feel they want to follow their heart with you, they may be steered by outside influences to sign with other programs – only to change their mind after a year or two.

These type of two- or three-year players need to be an exceptional fit for your program and ready to step into a starting role, in order for you to take them. They need to be physically and academically ready. They need to be able to step into starting jobs or be able to provide steady, productive minutes once they are eligible.

If they must redshirt for a year, be sure to put together a plan for them that will lead them into a starting job the minute they are eligible for competition.

EVALUATIONS: GATHERING VIDEO

A habit to develop in every initial conversation with recruits and prep coaches is to always ask for video. You need to be gathering as much potential quality video that you can, especially for underclassmen.

Video will be the biggest tool you'll have off-the-road to evaluate potential prospects. You need to dedicate time each day to watching it, so make it a regular habit of gathering video for quality prospects.

As a staff, have a system for video to funnel through so that everyone receives a response—even if just an email to make them aware of your camp or to send a link to your online questionnaire.

Remember, it takes time to put together a quality collection of video to evaluate. Work ahead so your video operations staff is able to piece them together so the staff can evaluate prospects together early!

EVALUATIONS: TIME MANAGEMENT BEFORE WATCHING PROSPECT'S VIDEO

The #1 rule I preach to recruits is that for a college coach to have a legitimate interest in recruiting them, the coach must see them play and evaluate them athletically-- either in person or on video. I tell them that any conversation coaches have with them before getting a chance to see them play is out of politeness, unless they have great size.

One of the biggest time-savers you need to learn is to convey this to all of the unsolicited callers and office visitors (and the emailers and letter writers) that get in front of you, and send them on their way with the ball in their court. Throughout your day, you will get prep players, parents and prep coaches visiting campus who stop by the office, stop you in the grocery store, stop you in the airport. Calls, letters and emails are pouring in-- mostly from players you've never heard of through your research. At some schools, you could devote a full-time person to simply respond to these prospects, give quick facility tours and answer their questions -- and still not have enough time to respond to everyone. It's a struggle, because as a great recruiter you want everyone to walk away from your program with a positive experience.

DON'T HAVE THE BUDGET TO PRINT AND MAIL QUESTIONNAIRES TO DISTRIBUTE UNLIMITEDLY? CREATE AN ONLINE VERSION WITH A FREE GOOGLE DRIVE ACCOUNT THAT CAN BE EMAILED AND LINKED FROM YOUR WEBSITE. AS A BONUS, THE RESULTS ARE AUTOMATICALLY DOWNLOADED INTO AN EXCEL SPREADSHEET, MAKING FOR AN EASY CAMP MAILOUT.

You need a script... fast!

Quickly develop the skill of getting in and out of these intro conversations with, "Sure, let's get a chance to evaluate you– send me your video or maybe you can get to one of our camps." Give them a questionnaire and your personal business card, and send them on their way within a minute or less.

IF SOMEONE GETS TO YOU PITCHING THEMSELVES, THEY WILL TALK AS LONG AS YOU LET THEM! YOU NEED TO LEARN TO QUICKLY GET OUT OF THESE SITUATIONS IN THE POLITEST WAY POSSIBLE!

If your staff gets hundreds of inquiries weekly – have generic cards made up for the office with a generic email or phone number that can be routed to grad assistants or other staff.

Some of these players who find you and approach you first can definitely play, and may end up being part of your program. Just because you haven't heard of them (yet) doesn't mean they can't make a significant impact for you. Others-- they may be dreaming, but have somehow gotten in front of you, pitching themselves to their "dream school." Regardless-- it's worth your time to be polite, give them the next step and move on. But you have to master this conversation to only take a few seconds of your time. They will talk as long as you will let them!

RESOURCES (TIME, KNOWLEDGE AND MONEY) NEED TO BE RESERVED FOR PLAYERS WITH THE BIGGEST POTENTIAL PAYOFF. LEARN TO POLITELY LIMIT YOUR TIME WITH PLAYERS WHO WILL NEVER MAKE THE CUT WITHIN YOUR PROGRAM.

If you are approached by someone who passes the eye test, it never hurts to spend a few extra minutes with them. Ask them if they have any offers yet or who have they been receiving interest from? Pick up the phone and call their prep coach or YouTube/Google them after they leave. A great player may have just fallen in your lap, and even better- they already have interest in your program! Some may impress you off the bat, but looks never guarantee skill!

YOU MUST SET UP A SYSTEM THAT WILL MINIMIZE YOUR PERSONAL TIME ON UNSOLICITED CONTACTS, BUT MAXIMIZE A GREAT IMPRESSION.

#1 - BE POLITE
#2 - GIVE A QUESTIONNAIRE AND BUSINESS CARD
#3 - TELL THEM TO SEND YOU THEIR VIDEO
#4 - DIRECT THEM TO YOUR CAMPS AS AN OPTION
#5 - MOVE ON!

Make sure that your grad assistants and interns can give a quick tour of the facilities, and even a more extended tour with in-depth info and extra stops for more promising prospects. Motivate grad assistants by reinforcing the importance of this opportunity, that you are giving them an impactful responsibility. Let them give non-priority recruits and unexpected visitors quick facility tours to help train them for Unofficial/Official Visit weekends.

Have a grad assistant or staffer drop a questionnaire in the mail (or email if financially tight) to all of those prospects who reached out to you via mail or email. A nice gesture goes a long way, and puts the ball in the prospects court. In the long run, it's always a good idea to make a good impression with everyone along the way– you never know where it will lead down the recruiting road.

EVALUATIONS: FIT FOR HEAD COACH

As an assistant coach you may have aspirations to be a head coach one day— even one day very soon. You're sure to have a vision of how you would build your team, your style of play and the type of recruits you'd go after. You've likely daydreamed for decades about how you will run your team.

Press pause on those thoughts, at least while you're recruiting as an assistant coach!

When recruiting players in your current position you must identify and pursue prospects who are a good fit for your head coach's system—not your personal philosophy or style of play. If you have a great relationship with your head coach, they may ask for your input and take your recommendations. But when thinking of the big picture of the type of recruits that you will pursue, always defer to your head coach's vision.

To succeed, there can only be one vision– the head coach's vision. You can't build a successful team if everyone is doing it their way!

Your job as an assistant coach is to help your head coach succeed in their plan and system. You are there to help them look good. As a staff, the head coach needs to dictate position-by-position the skills, physical attributes and intangibles they're looking for to fit their style of play, and as a staff, you must stick to that script when recruiting players!

Over the years, visualize the team that you would like to build, go ahead and detail your vision. Keep files, write down your plan, allow yourself to dream-- but keep your personal vision on the back burner until you've been given the keys to your own ride! Focus on the direction your head coach wants and recruit those type of players.

EVALUATIONS: HOW TO BE A GREAT EVALUATOR OF TALENT — QUALITIES TO LOOK FOR

You need to streamline position-by-position, your evaluations and put all prospects through the same evaluation criteria. How do they stack up by position among each other?

Put together a form for each primary recruiting coach to fill out for group staff evaluations. When you begin to evaluate positions and depth chart needs, you need to detail strengths, weaknesses, projections and academic notes to give a complete picture of each player to the staff.

Player: Jeff Miles
Position: WR
High School (City): Northeast HS (Houston, TX)
Measurables: 6'2" – 170 – 4.5 (Include how measurable verified, if submitted by coach or gathered from combine source)
Strengths: Great burst, above average mechanics. No problem going across middle. Competitive.
Weaknesses: Gets down on self after drop. Needs to improve strength. Can get frustrated easily.
Possible Other Positions: Safety
Development Plan: Redshirt Freshman. Contribute as R-Freshman, Sophomore. Start as Junior.
Academics: Should have no academic eligibility issues. Is on track.
Notes: Father played at Mississippi State and coaches at Greenbriar JC. Attended camp last summer.

It's also important as a staff to sit down and make a detailed list – position by position -- of the key characteristics and measurements that you're looking for. Every assistant coach needs to have a grasp on each position's needs when making initial evaluations in their assigned regions.

When doing evaluations you will need to look for players that fit the head coach's vision. You are looking for players who can be successful in your head coach's system, within the conference and within the team's culture (or the culture your head coach is trying to build).

<u>**Each category can key in on a few traits, or more detailed with 5-8 qualities:**</u>
    • **SKILL:** Position-by-position, what is the staff looking for? Footwork, routes, shot selection, steals, rebounds, mechanics, hands, win one-on-one, makes plays in traffic, ball security, blocking, takes great angles, reads coverages, ball skills, athletic, position fundamentals, disruptive on ball, etc.

    • **SPEED:** What exact measureables will they need to be competitive or successful within the conference? Initial burst, 40-yard, first step, explosiveness, quickness, acceleration, change of direction, second gear, lateral speed, closing burst, etc.

    • **SIZE:** What height and weight ranges will they need in order to be competitive within the conference? Height, weight, body composition, % body fat, frame, long arms, big hands, etc.

- **WEIGHT ROOM:** Which weight room test numbers will help them be successful within the conference? Leaping ability, bench press, core strength, upper body strength, lower body strength, balance, power, vertical jump, flexibility, conditioning, endurance, etc.

- **INTANGIBLES:** "Difference Makers" – What culture are you trying to build? What traits are the most important -- leadership, toughness, competitiveness, attitude, game IQ, decision making, poise, confidence, energy, maturity, patience, coachable, courageous, fearless, good motor, love for the game, team player, aggressive to ball, communicator. Can they be trusted?

- **ACADEMICS:** Based on University standards, can they be admitted and will they be successful there? Will they have constant eligibility issues?

- **RED FLAGS:** What won't you put up with? Do they take plays off, play soft, get frustrated easily, are indecisive, whine, make excuses, are disrespectful, don't take school serious, have a negative attitude, are selfish, blame others, mentally weak, undisciplined, complains to the refs, have been arrested, etc?

- **INJURIES:** Have they had serious injuries in the past? Are they prone to minor injuries? Do they miss games due to injuries?

EVALUATIONS: RANKING YOUR 'WATCH LIST'
Not every recruit is created equal! Not every recruit on your list will receive the same level of attention, invites and mail.

Most staffs have a ranking system within their prospect database, a way to rate recruits by their ability or by the level of attention that they want to give them in terms of mail (form letters or hand-written notes), email, calls and what events they get invited to.

COMMON GROUPS INCLUDE:
- Current commitments
- Top priorities to get a commitment from next (wish list of top recruits)
- Players who are being actively recruited, who likely have offers
- Plan B Players (backup plans or players who may be out-of-reach)
- Top Underclassmen who are too young to be contacted
- Players who were evaluated earlier and labeled 'not talented enough at this time'
- Players who coaches were previously interested in, who committed to other schools

RECRUITING DOESN'T END EVEN AFTER A PLAYER COMMITS!

Most commonly, each assistant coach has a top list of players that they are 'actively recruiting.' Depending on what time of year it is and where they are in the recruiting cycle, this is the list of prospects that they will regularly call, visit, do research on and try to get to campus for an Unofficial or Official Visit. 'Actively recruiting' is the key phrase, and this group includes players who have already committed, players who have already been offered a scholarship or players who are on the verge of getting an offer.

VISUALLY, HAVE A BOARD THAT LISTS TOP RECRUITS POSITION-BY-POSITION, IN ORDER OF PREFERENCE. THIS LIST WILL CHANGE REGULARLY AS PROSPECTS BEGIN COMMITTING TO OTHER SCHOOLS OR ARE ELIMINATED AFTER YOUR EVALUATIONS. VISUALLY, RANK YOUR TOP CHOICES IN ORDER.

Beyond these players who are being actively recruited, there is often a B-list of players. These are prospects who could potentially be backup offers if the first, second, third or fourth choices don't work out. These prospects usually receive some mail, emails and who may get an invite to group Unofficial Visits, scrimmages or games. This list may also include players who coaches may think are unattainable, players who are long-shots that they may still check in with or mail information to, just hoping for a chance to get their foot in the door.

Beyond those two groups, coaches normally keep rankings of top players that have committed to other schools and prospects that they determined are currently not talented enough for their program in the database under another ranking. Never delete prospects entirely from your database, rather just give them an inactive ranking since the statuses of players often changes— players decommit from other universities, get better, have a growth spurt or re-classify grades. I've seen many players cut from 'Actively Recruiting' lists who re-surfaced months later and were added back on, even eventually earning scholarship offers.

NEVER DELETE PROSPECTS ENTIRELY FROM YOUR DATABASE, RATHER JUST GIVE THEM AN INACTIVE RANKING SINCE THE STATUSES OF PLAYERS OFTEN CHANGES— PLAYERS DECOMMIT FROM OTHER UNIVERSITIES, GET BETTER, HAVE A GROWTH SPURT OR RE-CLASSIFY GRADES.

Each sport varies, some coaches deactivate players who have verbally committed to other programs off their recruiting lists immediately. Other sports continue to recruit, send mail and invite to visit campus as verbal commitments are non-binding, and often ever-changing. Take direction from your head coach as it ultimately reflects on your program. Does the head coach want you to deactivate players that have committed to other schools from mailing lists or continue to contact and send information as normal?

DEVELOP A RANKING SYSTEM FOR YOUR PLAYERS:

- **A's or 1's** – Offers / Head Coach recruiting (Receive all event invites, receive hand-written mail, receive most communication pieces)
- **B's or 2's** – Potential Offers – Players who would be able to compete in your conference (Receive all event invites, receive some hand-written mail, receive some communication pieces)
- **C's or 3's** – Plan B's – Players who may be able to compete within the conference or could be preferred walk-ons (Receive general event invites, receive general communications and form letters)
- **D's or 4's** – Not recruiting at this time (Have committed to other programs, aren't good enough at this time, have red flags)
- **E's or 5's** – Potential walk-on players

Have every coach use this same system to code players, and have a category in your database to include this ranking. Give standards of which players would fit into each of these categories so each coach is using the same standard ranking system.

For scholarship offers, develop a system of who will send offer letters out with head coach's approval, which coaches will receive notice of offers sent out and who will keep track of all offers sent.

EVALUATIONS: EVALUATING INTANGIBLES

Stats, measurables and video can tell you a lot—but the ultimate difference-maker when evaluating players is understanding and confirming intangibles. Every championship-caliber player and coach that I've worked for has had strong intangibles. Discuss as a staff the top 5-10 characteristics you would like for your team to play with. Great qualities to look for beyond position skill, size and speed:

> **WHEN DISCUSSING YOUR TOP TARGETS WITH PREP COACHES AND YOUR SOURCES IN THE AREA, FIND OUT MORE ABOUT WHAT INTANGIBLES THEY COMPETE WITH. INTANGIBLES SEPARATE GOOD PLAYERS FROM GREAT ONES!**

INTANGIBLES TO LOOK FOR:
- Makes good decisions
- Poised
- Competitive
- Wants the ball when the game is on the line
- Hard worker
- Tough
- Fiery leader
- Confident
- Natural instincts
- Patient
- Focused
- Mature
- Coachable
- Great motor
- Love for the game

- Doesn't make the same mistake twice
- Team Player
- Aggressive
- Has a presence
- Recovers from mistakes
- Great energy
- Good communicator

RECRUIT THE INTANGIBLES THAT YOU ARE MISSING AS A TEAM. TREAT THE PROBLEMS IN YOUR HUDDLE OR LOCKERROOM.

EVALUATIONS: EVALUATING RISK VS. REWARD

One of the toughest aspects of evaluating top players is analyzing risk versus reward, if you encounter red flags during your research.

You will likely come across players who can be big playmakers for you-- everything impresses you-- until you start getting info that they have major legal, drug, attitude, academic or family issues.

Are you willing to take a high-risk (and high-maintenance) player who is very talented... or would you rather give up some of the drama and stress and take a player who is a little less talented but more dependable? Will this potential top recruit negatively influence and impact your team chemistry and lockerroom, will they bring other players down with them? Could they potentially cost you your job?

Ultimately, it's the head coaches and Athletic Director's decision when it comes to signing or even recruiting red-flag players. As a staff, you need to discuss what will and what won't be accepted-- and go ahead and eliminate those prospects who don't fit your staff's (and university's) standards early and move on!

Character is a key component to trust—and trust is essential if you want to win. You have to be able to trust your team, so recruit with this in mind.

Not only do you need to consider the prospect, you need to take a look at their parents and circle of close friends, mentors and family. Once enrolled, they will have numerous people in their ears-- will they be positive or negative influences? Is the player easily influenced by this circle, or are they looking to stand on their own? Will their parents be complaining about playing time, influencing the player's attitude? Will their parents be calling your office weekly or daily, trying to tell you how to do your job? How parents carry themselves during the recruiting process only gets magnified once their child is enrolled -- are you ready to take them on as well?

Players CAN change-- but it's a game of chances and only capable within a small percentage of people. These are the type of gambles that can disrupt your career, if big enough. Players can change if their motivation is big enough-- their love for the game, an education, draft chances... I've seen players mature under the right leadership. But for many players, it's a long, rough road to get there, and sometimes only a temporary change. Does this player bring the strengths that would make it worth dedicating that much extra time and effort on?

> **NOTHING SLOWS DOWN AN ORGANIZATION MORE THAN PARALYSIS BY ANALYSIS—THE INABILITY TO MAKE SMALL DECISIONS QUICKLY. A SIMPLE SET OF GUIDELINES THAT ARE SHARED BY EVERYONE WITHIN THE ORGANIZATION HELP FOR FASTER DECISIONS. VISION CHANGES NOTHING, BUT GUIDELINES FOR QUICK DECISIONS DO CHANGE ORGANIZATIONS!**
>
> -FROM *IT'S NOT THE BIG THAT EAT THE SMALL... IT'S THE FAST THAT EAT THE SLOW*

Take a page from NFL scouts: they ask receptionists, lunch ladies, trainers, coaches, stadium security guards and anyone else that a player may come in contact with to find out their true colors—not just how they act around coaches or perform on the field. An NFL prospects 'true colors' are almost as important as their athletic ability when it comes to breaking down the top talent. How is the player mentally, spiritually and what type of person are they? How do they handle success, how do they handle adversity? NFL teams are making decisions between players and investing millions and millions of dollars into their draft picks—they need to know about every aspect of their life. YOU should take that same consideration when evaluating players. Sometimes it's more about what they're not telling you that you need to look into. Do your research!

> **BEING A COLLEGE COACH IS NOW A 24-HOUR-A-DAY-JOB-- YOU WILL BE RESPONSIBLE FOR THIS PLAYER FOR THE NEXT FEW YEARS, ON AND OFF-THE-FIELD. ARE YOU WILLING TO DEAL WITH THEM EVERY DAY? WILL YOU BE GETTING THOSE MIDNIGHT CALLS ABOUT A FIGHT, A LEGAL INCIDENT, AN ACCIDENT?**

THOUGHTS TO CONSIDER:
- Will the prospect negatively impact the chemistry or personality of your team and lockerroom? Will they peer pressure other players into trouble?
- Have they had issues in the past? Have they changed their ways and stayed clean over the last year or two?
- Will they be admitted into the University and be able to actually enroll? Do you think they'll make it through Academics, Compliance and Admissions approvals?

- Can they be successful there outside of sports? Will they be able to make it through their freshman and sophomore years? If redshirting, can they stay out of trouble the year that they're on the bench?
- Are they likely to embarrass the University or program?
- Will you have to pull teeth each step of the way to get them to go to class or turn in papers? Academic problems are often more of an issue of effort, not necessarily intelligence. Will you be babysitting them daily to do their homework?
- Most likely, issues become even more magnified when they move to the bigger stage of college sports. Can they handle it?
- Are you willing to put up with their parents and mentors for four years? What "mentors" are around them?
- Are they bringing a negative circle of friends with them? Will they be bringing negativity to your community?
- Will you be getting 2am phone calls about this player being in trouble?
- When discussing their past, are they just telling you what you want to hear or do you think they can now be trusted?
- What attitude do they have on social media? How do they carry themselves around peers?

A COMMON MISTAKE YOUNG COACHES MAKE IS TO WASTE TOO MUCH TIME RECRUITING A PLAYER WHO WILL NEVER MAKE IT WITHIN THEIR PROGRAM!

EVALUATIONS: BUILDING A TEAM

As you are filling each position need, you also have to remember that you are building a TEAM, an organization that requires everyone to work as one in order to succeed. It may take time for these friendships to gel, but do you have the pieces that can come together?

You don't need matching personalities or backgrounds but you need players who can mesh together. Players who can get along, who you can piece together into one unit.

Envision your lockerroom and their personalities, who can you ultimately win a championship with? Can you trust your recruits? Are they goal-driven and team-oriented?

Be sure to dedicate focus on building team chemistry and encourage off-the-field and court relationships and activities. Even encourage your signees to begin communicating and getting to know each other, the earlier everyone can come together the better!

EVALUATIONS: SCHOLARSHIP OFFERS
Articulate as a staff the scholarship offer process. Video is evaluated, in order by:

- Recruiting Coach
- Position Coach
- By entire coaching staff
- By the Head Coach. After recommendations and review, the Head Coach makes final decision on scholarship offer.
- Offer extended in writing from Head Coach's office
- Recruiting Coordinator, Recruiting Coach and Position Coach notified and sent a copy of offer letter
- A full "Offers & Commitments" file or board –with a goal of number of signees expected position-by-position – needs to be updated immediately and visible to all staffers.

EVALUATIONS: CAN THEY BE SUCCESSFUL WITHIN THE CURRENT SYSTEM, PROGRAM AND UNIVERSITY?

Transfers are inevitable—they happen in every program and under every head coach. As you are evaluating players from every angle – take a good look at the probability that they can be successful within your system, under that head coach, at that school and in that town.

Players transfer for a variety of reasons—they're too far from home; they aren't getting enough playing time; they don't mesh with the coaching staff or lockerroom; they face too many challenges academically and have a difficult time staying eligible; or their athletic strengths can't be utilized in the current system. For most transfers, they fall into one of those categories.

And many transferring players knew these issues existed before they committed and enrolled, and so did many of their recruiting coaches. Take a good look at these factors and even bring it up to the prospect if things are getting serious, and you have a feeling it may not work out in the long run.

As you build relationships with prospects and their families, you will be able to gauge if they'll be a good fit in the lockerroom and under the coaching staff.

Transfers can't be avoided 100% of the time, but in a many cases there were red flags leading up to enrollment. With maturity that comes along with the college experience, some of these issues can be overcome. But for some players, it just wasn't a good fit for them from the beginning. Will they be in over their head or doomed from the beginning?

When players are happy they play well, their attitudes lift the team up. When they're frustrated about playing time, having personality clashes with teammates and coaches or constantly falling behind in academics, they'll drag negative energy to your lockerroom and disrupt team chemistry.

As you evaluate players, you must go beyond 40 times, verticals and stats—you must evaluate them as a person as a whole and visualize them in your lockerroom, team meeting room, huddle, campus and position group. Is the "fit" good for both the player and coaching staff? Will they be happy there?

Part of building a great reputation among prep coaches is being honest, and looking out for the prospect as much as you're looking out for yourself.

One of the most successful staffs that I've worked for didn't make decisions based on what was best for them, they always looked out for the player and did what was best for them in the long run. That type of integrity is respected among prep coaches and builds a reputation of trust, and word spreads. Ultimately, you want to be trusted among prep coaches in this area.

RANKING PLAYERS: DO THEY REALLY WANT TO BE HERE?
Although it shouldn't necessarily help a player get their foot in the door, a player who is passionate about your program should weigh into recruiting evaluations when deciding between offering great prospects.

Ask yourself, "Do they REALLY want to be here?" Are they excited about our program? Are they excited about the opportunity? Will they take great pride in their opportunities? Do they have family ties to the University?

Once on campus, other players may chase the social scene, run home at every chance or become easily distracted off-the-field. You're looking for players who take great pride in your program, players who are excited to be a part of it and who really want to be there!

EVALUATIONS: TRAVEL PLANS
To make the most of your evaluation days and recruit travel, you need an organized plan. Since head coaches often are accompanied by an assistant coach or assistant coaches visit prospects together, detailed travel itineraries are essential to avoid confusion and wasting time. The more lead time you have to book flights, the better rates you can lock in. As a staff, you should sit down prior to major evaluation periods to plan out visits and prospects you want to have multiple coaches visit or evaluate.

PUT TOGETHER A VERY DETAILED CALENDAR INCLUDING:
- Day-by-day, who is required to be off the road?
- Which assistants will be traveling together on what dates, evaluating which prospects?
- Who will be traveling with the head coach on which dates, evaluating which prospects?
- Who will be using university transportation? Who will be renting transportation, coordinating flights, booking hotels?
- For coaches off the road, what are their responsibilities while others are out?

As an assistant coach, work at least a few days out. Call prep coaches 2-3 days ahead of time to set a specific meeting time and location. Find out what a good time for THEM would be, try to work around their schedule. If necessary, confirm the address and their cell phone number, so you can contact them if you are delayed.

Never leave a school empty-handed, bring back transcripts, correct spelling of prospect and coach names, evaluation notes, contact information, video. Always leave your business card, camp brochures and questionnaires.

When traveling with the head coach, and if possible for yourself, put together an itinerary with all necessary information: coaches traveling, flight information, directions, addresses, confirmation numbers, reservations, travel time, game times, meeting times, jersey numbers of prospects, etc.

EXAMPLE:

Coach Thomas Itinerary
Thursday, October 1st

Recruiting with Coach Johnson: Coach Thomas and Coach Walker

8:00PM – Depart University after practice
9:30PM – Flight departs (American Airlines Flight #9895)
10:45PM – Arrive in Atlanta
      Car: Avis Airport
                Confirmation #: 38488488383

      Hotel: Hilton Garden Inn 404-555-5555
                1245 Peachtree Street, Atlanta, GA 30308
                Confirmation #: 8493930203948

RECRUITING MADE SIMPLE

Friday, October 2nd
**Directions attached

8AM - North High School – 217 Northwest 13th Street
Coach: Mike Smith - 404-556-7878
Recruits: Kevin Thompson, Paul Jackson, Chris Avery

(15 minute drive)

10AM - Greentree High School – 455 Southwest 45th Street
Coach: Angel Fernandez - 404-755-8787
Recruits: Lorento Solomon, Phillip Allen, Shannard Kelly

(22 minute drive)

1PM - Sheridan High School – 23 Fairfield Avenue
Coach: Courtney Dunham - 404-345-9000
Recruits: Dwayne Cohen, Billy Lewis

(20 minute drive)

6:45-PM - Westline vs. Southlake game at Westline HS (7:00PM kickoff)

Westline HS	Southlake HS
Rob Thompson – (OL) #75	Michael Hampton – (DL) #57
Kelvin Jefferson – (TE) #83	Roger West – (WR) #12
Jorge Rivera – (DB) #21	

8:30PM – Depart Westline High School

(7 minute drive)

8:45PM – Arrive ATL Airport
10:00PM – Depart ATL – American Airlines Flt #4534
11:15PM – Arrive Home Airport

BE EXTREMELY DETAILED IN TRAVEL PLANS TO ELIMINATE ANY CONFUSION OR MISTAKES, ESPECIALLY WHEN COORDINATING TRAVEL WITH YOUR HEAD COACH OR OTHER ASSISTANT COACHES. DETAIL EACH LEG, WHO WILL BE TRAVELING ON EACH LEG, CONTACT PHONE NUMBERS, ADDRESSES, DEPARTURE TIMES, TRAVEL TIMES, CONFIRMATION NUMBERS AND DIRECTIONS.

CHAPTER #4
ACADEMICS

"It's the little details that are vital. Little things make big things happen."
-JOHN WOODEN

"Concentrate on one goal. Nobody ever reached their potential by scattering themselves in 20 directions. Reaching your potential requires focus."
-JOHN C. MAXWELL

"Leadership is a matter of having people look at you and gain confidence…If you're in control, they're in control."
-TOM LANDRY

"The quality of a leader is reflected in the standards they set for themselves."
-RAY KROC

ACADEMICS: KNOW SAT/ACT DATES

Know upcoming SAT/ACT dates and proactively encourage your priority recruits to register and prepare for the tests early.

<u>REMIND PROSPECTS THAT:</u>

- The ACT and SAT both offer free practice tests online, encourage prospects to take prior to the real test.
- The ACT and SAT both offer free practice "Questions of the Day" on Twitter! Follow @ACTStudent and @OfficialSAT for daily practice questions.
- Fee waivers are available for low-income students in 11th and 12th grade that cover testing fees and sending scores to four colleges. Have prospects speak with their guidance counselor to request a waiver.
- Procrastinating taking the tests can result in failure to qualify, and if late enough, failure to enroll.

When speaking with families and players, remind them about registration deadlines that are nearing! Always be aware of when the next test deadline registration is, and advise players to test early. Post ACT/SAT test dates and registration deadlines near your phone, visible when making calls. Remind them to use code 9999 to have scores sent directly to the NCAA or 9876 to have scores sent to the NAIA.

ACADEMICS: YOUR PLAYERS IMPROVE

Similar to showing that your players improve on-field, it's important to track their academic and off-field improvements as well. Are their GPA's improving? Can you show position GPA increases and team GPA increases semester-to-semester or year-to-year? Can you increase your number of Athletic Department or Conference Academic Honor Roll honorees? Track and improve these academic numbers for added recruiting power, be just as prideful of these achievements as you are of athletic improvements!

> **BE JUST AS PRIDEFUL OF ACADEMIC ACHIEVEMENTS AS YOU ARE OF ATHLETIC IMPROVEMENTS!**

And as you take an active role in their on-field daily activities, you will have to put that same effort into their academic life. You can't sit back and wait for a call at the end of the semester from their academic counselor telling you that a player is academically ineligible. You have to have weekly (or sometimes daily) check-ins on the academic progress of your position players.

Set up a weekly meeting with your players regularly to have realistic conversations about their academics. Look your players in their eyes and let them know that you are serious and dedicated to their academic success.

ACADEMIC MENTORING:

- Get a copy of each position player's class schedule, blocked out on a weekly schedule, so you know where they are at any time of day.
- For at-risk or all players, do daily or random attendance checks by showing up at their classroom before class starts.
- For each player, get a copy of their syllabus for each class they're enrolled in. Add test dates or paper deadlines to your calendar and check in with them days before to see how they're preparing and to make sure they're on track.
- Set up weekly meetings with academic counselors working with your players. Make sure they feel welcome to call you with issues. Make sure academic counselors working with your players have your cell phone number and feel welcome to call you, especially before they become big issues.
- Make sure your team academic counselors know to alert you immediately of any red flags or academic issues with your players
- Be aware of class registration deadlines and procedures. Sit down with your players to discuss registration decisions for the next semester.
- Be sure that you are alerted that day when a player has an unexcused class absence.

AS YOU BUILD YOUR CAREER, MAKE IT A PRIORITY TO HELP YOUR PLAYERS ACHIEVE ACADEMIC GOALS. TRACK TEAM GPA'S, POSITION GROUP GPA'S, PLAYERS GRADUATED, NUMBER OF PLAYERS OVER A 3.0/3.5 GPA, PLAYERS IN GRADUATE PROGRAMS. TRACK ACADEMICS SEMESTER-BY-SEMESTER AND YEAR-BY-YEAR TO SHOW IMPROVEMENTS WITHIN THE PROGRAM UNDER YOUR DIRECTION.

Acknowledge your players achievements academically, however small they may initially be. Reward the behaviors you want to see repeated and duplicated by other players!

Prepare your new signees for the transition from high school to college. Are they ready for their heavier course load with additional freedoms? Do you have mandatory study hall hours for freshmen and at-risk players based on GPA?

Your players may be unappreciative and fighting it now, but in 10-20 years they'll appreciate the effort and attention you put into their academics more than anything you will do for them athletically.

ACADEMICS: UNDERSTANDING YOUR UNIVERSITY ADMISSIONS POLICIES

A huge resource-waster for you: putting a ton of travel time and money into recruiting a player who will never be admitted into the University. Every Admissions Office is different. Each school varies greatly on their admissions standards and how flexible they are with the Athletic Department.

IF A PLAYER YOU REALLY WANT IS ACADEMICALLY BORDERLINE: HOLD OFF ON SUBMITTING THEIR TRANSCRIPT UNTIL YOU HAVE TO. THE UNIVERSITY OR ATHLETIC DEPARTMENT MAY DISCOURAGE YOU OR ASK YOU TO END THEIR RECRUITMENT IF THEY FEEL THEY'RE TOO AT-RISK.

When you take a new job you need to immediately find out:

#1- What are the minimum requirements to be admitted to the University (may be higher than NCAA Sliding Scale requirements)

#2- How flexible is the University with the Athletic Department when admitting players of your sport?

If you are at an academically-tough university that doesn't allow for much extra consideration on admissions decisions, decide early about how much time you will put into recruiting upperclassmen who may have too much ground to make up academically, in a year or two.

Most universities have a designated liaison between Admissions and the Athletic Department, so coaches normally communicate with their internal Athletic Department liaison, who will communicate with the University directly. Speak directly through your Athletic Department contact, it's not common or recommended for coaches to communicate with Admissions directly.

When identifying players for potential scholarship offers, work quickly to get a copy of their unofficial transcript to get a true picture of where the player is at-- don't just take their coach's word for it. If you're slightly interested, request a copy of their transcript!

SOME UNIVERSITIES MAKE NO EXCEPTIONS FOR ATHLETES WHO DON'T QUALIFY UNDER GENERAL ADMISSIONS GUIDELINES WHILE OTHER UNIVERSITIES MAY BARELY SET A MINIMUM STANDARD AND ALLOW NEARLY ANYONE IN, IF REQUESTED. FIND OUT WHAT THE MINIMUM STANDARDS ARE AT YOUR UNIVERSITY. YOU DON'T WANT TO WASTE A SCHOLARSHIP ON A PLAYER WHO WILL EVENTUALLY FAIL TO ENROLL DAYS OR WEEKS BEFORE THE SEMESTER STARTS!

You also need to evaluate if the recruit has enough credits to be on track to graduate, what are their deficiencies? Evaluate their Core Course GPA (see page

62) and see if their ACT/SAT test scores are available and if they're qualifying. Are their SAT/ACT scores borderline qualifying or do they have great scores? If they haven't taken the ACT or SAT yet or if scores are significantly low—reinforce the importance of taking the tests soon to the prospect, their parents and their coach. SAT/ACT scores are often the final hurdle needed to get through the NCAA Eligibility Center and Admissions Department, and players can be rejected after signing their NLIs.

Sit down with your Athletic Department Compliance Office and Academics Office to get familiar with the basic policies and procedures of the department so that you aren't tripped up later by high standards. Remember, TIME is your most valuable resource, don't waste it on players who will never qualify!

GET TO KNOW THE ACADEMICS OF YOUR TOP RECRUITS EARLY! GET UNOFFICIAL TRANSCRIPTS, CORE COURSE GPA'S AND THEIR SAT/ACT SCORES NOW! OUTLINE THEIR CORE COURSE DEFICIENCIES AND SAT/ACT SCORE GOALS TO GET AN IDEA OF HOW CLOSE THEY ARE TO QUALIFYING!

ACADEMICS: UNDERSTANDING YOUR UNIVERSITY ACADEMIC SELLING POINTS

Since academics are a key decision factor for most parents, and for some prospects, get to know key selling points for both the University and the Athletic Department. You want to have your facts straight and be well-versed in your campus knowledge! Have your staff take an official campus tour through the Admissions Office every year or six months to learn more about new upgrades, technology, campus initiatives or buildings.

Many players may be intimidated by college curriculum-- do you have good technology, tutor programs, internship opportunities? What separates your Athletic Department from others in terms of academic support? Most schools have similar programs and assistance, is there anything that your school does better or differently? Do your student-athletes have unique opportunities in the town that you are located in or with alumni programs across the country? Do you have current players or recent grads who participated in unique internships or programs?

Get to know what majors are popular among your players. What are the most interesting five to ten majors on your campus?

Perception is reality—what is the most common reaction that you hear from prospects, parents and coaches about your university? Do those common perceptions match the facts that you know about your university? How can you change opinions about your university with the best academic facts about your university?

See page 121 for more academic selling points!

ACADEMICS: LIKELIHOOD OF GRADUATION
A common philosophy that many great coaches have is to primarily recruit players who have a high likelihood of graduating from the University. If not, it's a stressful life working with a roster full of players who are borderline-eligible every semester. The stress is often not worth it!

Ultimately, you want to be able to recruit players who will transition to campus, that won't need to be pushed or babysat every step of the way. You don't want a roster full of players who can't handle the work load or who can't stay eligible. Consider the academic resources and support that you are able to provide, and if they will have issues beyond that.

Sure, there are special cases, particular players will need extra academic attention from your staff. But at the end of the day, the ultimate goal is to recruit players that you can provide an excellent college playing experience to, and players who have an opportunity to earn a college degree.

ACADEMICS: INVOLVE UNIVERSITY FACULTY MEMBERS
When taking over jobs and working at new universities, develop contacts within the popular majors of your players and prospects. Take the time to find just the right professors or deans who would be able to meet with prospects during Official and Unofficial Visits. Ask your academic counselors for direction on which professors the Athletic Department has had success working with, and ask your players for recommendations on their favorite faculty. You need to find great faculty ambassadors for your program who will be willing to be involved in recruiting.

When scheduling tours during Official and Unofficial Visits, include a meeting with a professor or the dean of the program that your prospect is interested in. Like coaches, not all professors have the personalities to "recruit." Professors or deans may be intimidating, too technical, poor at small talk, not interested in assisting Athletics. Take time to find the right people who can and want to be involved in your program.

START WITH THE TOP FIVE MAJORS AND WORK TO IDENTIFY GREAT AMBASSADORS WITHIN EVERY ACADEMIC PROGRAM.

Also be aware of professors or majors that may be too good to be true. You can't play naïve to the fact that certain professors allow student-athletes to pass their class with no work submitted and poor attendance. Don't put your career in the hands of a professor who is too good to be true.

Don't expect to make a Friday morning call and expect a professor to drop everything to meet with your prospect over the weekend or that day for an Official Visit. Don't pull the "favor for the Athletic Department" card and expect professors to stop what they're doing to help you, they have busy schedules as well. If you ask ahead of time and prepare, you will have more luck at getting a 'yes.' Respect their schedules, ask for their assistance in advance, prepare them with background info on the prospect and their family, thank them for their time, and include them in an occasional banquet or team event.

WHEN SETTING UP APPOINTMENT WITH FACULTY:
- Send them an email with the prospects' name, high school, desired major and any other important information.
- Also include the names and relationships of the prospects guests that will be traveling with them to campus.
- Get their cell phone number, in case there is a last minute issue that will cause a delay!
- Give them your cell phone number so they can call you if they'll be late.
- Be on time for all appointments!
- If running late, call them in advance and keep them updated. If a new time is inconvenient for them, try to reschedule for a time that would be convenient for them.
- Thank them for their time, every time! Don't take them for granted!
- Ask for improvements or input that they may be able to share about visits, or more about their program that could help in recruiting the player.

ACADEMICS: SCHOLARSHIP BREAKDOWN OF NEEDED ACADEMIC REQUIREMENTS

As you get more and more serious with committed players and potential scholarship offers, keep a file handy of all academic deficiencies for your top prospects.

Sure Athletic Department Academic or Compliance Offices review prospect transcripts for you, or you may need to do it for yourself—but you need an exact list of required courses still needed, projected grades needed and ACT/SAT test score requirements.

With your committed players and top targets, take the time to be sure they understand the Core Course requirements and ask if they need assistance making decisions for registration for their next semester.

You need to master the Eligibility Requirements of the NCAA and your University and put together a form that you can use to calculate these requirements.

CHECKLIST:
- Official Transcript received.
- Registered for the ACT/SAT test on _____.
- Taken the ACT/SAT test on _____.
- Registered with the NCAA Eligibility Center on _____.
- Test scores needed for projected final GPA.
- Class grades needed for completed test scores.

You need to know where all of your top targets stand in terms of likelihood that they will be able to enroll.

CHAPTER #5
RECUITING CYCLE

"Don't let making a living prevent you from making a life."
-JOHN WOODEN

"The test of a good coach is that when they leave, others will carry on successfully."
-UNKNOWN

"Management is doing things right; leadership is doing the right thing."
-PETER F. DRUCKER

"My responsibility is leadership and the minute I get negative, that is going to have an influence on my team."
-DON SHULA

RECRUITING CYCLE: YEAR-TO-YEAR
FRESHMEN:
- Begin collecting names and video through the 8 Ways to Discover Players (see page 15).

- Send questionnaires to prospects tipped off on from 8 Ways to Discover Players (see page 15).

- Send summer camp brochures to top freshmen and share your camp info with prep coaches of great sophomore players

- Work to have prep teams of great freshmen players attend your Team Camp

- If you have a good handle on your seniors, juniors and sophomores, visit the high schools of your top freshmen during evaluation periods

- Allow for some evaluation time of top underclassmen during tournaments or games, if time allows and you are at a good place with your upperclassmen evaluations.

- Request video on your top freshmen from prep coaches. Watch the best of the best of the freshmen class as a staff to decide on early potential scholarship offers.

- Call sources in key areas to find out about up-and-coming underclassmen prospects in the area.

SOPHOMORES:
- Continue to build your Watch List based off the 8 Ways to Discover Players (see page 15).

- Request video on your top sophomores from prep coaches. Watch the best of the best as a staff to decide on potential scholarship offers.

- Send questionnaires to players as they are added to your Watch List to begin gathering mailing addresses, cell phone numbers and email addresses.

- Visit the high schools of your top sophomores during evaluation periods

- Allow for some evaluation time of top underclassmen during tournaments or games, if time allows and you are at a good place with your upperclassmen evaluations.

- Send summer camp brochures to top sophomores and share your camp info with prep coaches of great sophomore players

- Work to have prep teams of great sophomore players attend your Team Camp

- Unofficial visits - Invite great top players to games, unofficial visits, etc through their high school / prep coach.

- Request unofficial transcripts of your top prospects after their sophomore year.

- Set a daily goal of the number of phone calls made to prep coaches of your top sophomore prospects. Encourage prep coaches to have their prospect call you whenever, since you are unable to call them. Remind them that you are unable to call prospects back, so keep calling!

- Call sources in key areas to find out about up-and-coming underclassmen prospects in the area.

JUNIORS:
- Continue to build your Watch List based off the 8 Ways to Discover Players (see page 15).

- Request video on your top juniors from prep coaches, Watch the players who could be potential scholarship players as a staff to decide on potential offers.

- Send questionnaires to players as they are added to Watch List to help collect mailing addresses, cell phone numbers and email addresses.

- Begin requesting unofficial transcripts for all players that you are adding to your priority Watch List. Gather transcripts when visiting high schools during evaluation periods.

- Once allowed, begin sending mailouts, emails and handwritten notes to your prospects. Set up a plan for how much and what type of weekly communications your prospects will receive, by ranking.

- Once allowed, begin making phone calls, texting prospects (if allowed). See page 117 on tips for conversations.

- Evaluate the transcripts of your top prospects to determine deficiencies for Core Course requirements. Get an idea of how close they are to achieving GPA/Test Score requirements in relation to their Core Course GPA.

- Call sources in key areas to get feedback on your top targets, don't just speak to the player's coach when getting recommendations. Find out what reputation the player has in the area.

- Send summer camp brochures and share dates of your camps with prep coaches of great junior players.

- Unofficial Visits - Invite great top players to games, early in the cycle. Coordinate Unofficial Visit events that are larger and more generic. For your top prospects, set other dates for events that are smaller and more intimate, to allow for more one-on-one time. Find out when your top recruits are able to visit campus.

- When allowed, send university admissions guidebook.

- For your scholarship offers, speak with them individually about coming to campus for an individual Unofficial Visit. What day would work for them?

- Mail an impressive packet of information on first day allowable to top juniors, introducing the program.

- Mail handwritten notes to parents and prep coaches of your top prospects.

RECRUITING MADE SIMPLE

- Add your prospects to social media and message on the first day allowed, even at the first minute allowed

- Email a personalized message on the first day allowed, even at the first minute allowed

- Remind recruits to register for the ACT/SAT. Encourage them to begin taking free practice tests available online.

- Remind recruits to send ACT/SAT test scores to the Eligibility Center directly (use code 9999 for NCAA schools and code 9876 for NAIA schools)

- Encourage recruits to register with the NCAA Eligibility Center, and remind them that fee waivers are available if they need them. Direct them to their coach or Academic Counselor to coordinate.

- Encourage rising juniors to attend your summer camps and clinics

- Set a daily goal of junior prospects and parents to call. Reach out to them as allowed, as well as their prep coaches.

- Invite and encourage your top prospects to get to campus, set up a date or event that they would like to attend to spend time with you and the team

- Send information on preferred majors to each of your top prospects. Find out what academic program they're interested in.

- If you haven't already, identify who will be helping the recruit with the decision and work on building relationships with them. Include them in key mailouts or send occasional or weekly handwritten notes.

- Get a grasp on red flags that particular recruits may have, and how they can be overcome. Start making decisions on how much time you will invest in prospects with red flags?

- Monitor social media accounts of your top targets. How do they carry themselves? Who are they associated with? What are they involved in?

SENIORS:
- Continue to build your Watch List based off the 8 Ways to Discover Players (see page 15).

- Request more video on your top seniors and potential offers

- Send questionnaires to players as they are added to your Watch List to help collect mailing addresses, cell phones, email addresses.

- Immediately request transcripts for all players you are adding to your priority Watch List. Gather when visiting high schools.

- Evaluate transcripts of your top prospects to determine deficiencies for Core Course requirements. Get an idea of how close they are to achieving GPA/Test Score requirements based on their Core Course GPA.

- Encourage recruits to register with the NCAA Eligibility Center, and remind them that a fee waiver is available if needed. Direct them to their prep coach or Academic Counselor for assistance.

- Monitor social media accounts of your top targets. How do they carry themselves? Who are they associated with? What are they involved in?

- Call sources in key areas to get feedback on your top targets, don't just speak to the player's coach. Gather as much information as possible from your trusted sources.

- Mail handwritten notes to your top targets, their parents and prep coaches

- Send summer camp brochures to rising seniors and share camp information with prep coaches of great senior players

- Unofficial Visits - Invite great top players to games, early in the cycle. Coordinate unofficial day events that are larger and more generic. For your top prospects, set other dates for events that are smaller and more intimate, to allow for more one-on-one time.

- Friend or follow seniors on social media as you add them to your Watch List

- Remind recruits to register for the ACT/SAT ASAP if they haven't earned qualifying scores yet

- Remind recruits to send ACT/SAT test scores to the Eligibility Center directly (use code 9999 for NCAA schools and code 9876 for NAIA schools)

- Encourage rising seniors to attend your summer camps, elite camps and clinics

- Set a daily goal of senior prospects and parents to call. Reach out to them as allowed, as well as their prep coaches.

- Invite and encourage your top prospects to get to campus, try to schedule a date or event that they would like to attend to spend time with you and the team

- With approval of the head coach, invite your top prospects to an Official Visit weekend. Begin coordinating early which time of year they would like to visit.

- Set up an in-home visit with the head coach and yourself at the prospects home.

- Send information on preferred majors for each of your top prospects. If you haven't already, find out which academic program interests them.

- If you haven't already, identify who will be helping the recruit with the decision and build a relationship with them. Include these key people in your best mailouts and send occasional handwritten notes to them.

- Investigate red flags particular recruits may have, and how they can be overcome. Make decisions on how much time you will invest in prospects with major red flags?

JUNIOR COLLEGE:
- Determine which positions are weaknesses for the next season or two? Which positions need an athlete who is ready to step in and start? Are you having a hard time finding a good fit for a position with the next class of available prep players?

- Research JuCo players at thin positions and evaluate for potential scholarships.

- Work to get Junior College athletes eligible to enter during January semester.

RECRUITING CYCLE: YEARLY SCHEDULE
As a staff, develop a sample yearly schedule of key responsibilities and goals.

Prepare as a staff to attack each period through the cycle aggressively!

- List of schools that have top players that need to be seen
- List of schools that you need to visit, that don't necessarily have top players now
- Top 25 prospects in your area
- Top 25 prospects at your position
- Mass video request periods
- Potential Official Visit weekends
- Potential Unofficial Visit weekends (large groups and small groups)
- Coaching Clinic dates
- AAU Tourney/Jamboree dates
- Camp dates

SELLING YOURSELF: TAKING OVER A NEW JOB
Your first few months on a new campus will be a blur—be sure to have a well-thought out plan for your first few days, weeks and months of what is of the utmost importance!

TIPS:
- Eliminate the unnecessary from your schedule. A few minutes here and there add up over the day and week. When you take over a program your only priorities are:
    - Your Family
    - Player Meetings
    - Team Chemistry
    - Offseason Workouts
    - Academic Staff Meetings
    - Meeting University Administration, Faculty and Leaders
    - Getting to Know Key Prep Coaches in State
    - Getting to Know Top Influential Boosters, Alumni and Former Players
    - Marketing Program Excitement and Rejuvenation of Fans and Ticket Holders
    - Media Meetings
    - Recruiting Plan
    - Budget Meetings
    - Scheduling

- Your players and staff mirror will your energy. Players love playing for coaches who are as energetic as they are, it motivates them. They'll step up their energy levels and play hard for you. Keep your energy positive.

- Set a goal number of daily calls to make to the following groups: prospects, prep coaches, boosters, former players. Prioritize who the most important contacts are that you need to reach out to immediately and within the first week.

- Don't diss the old coach, especially personally. Most players and staff have a personal relationship with them, and it's just not necessary. Simply say, "We're going to do things differently," if you feel the urge to take a shot at the former coaching staff. "This is how we're going to do it now."

- With your new current players, getting them to focus on attention to detail will be your top priority. Especially if you are walking into a program with a losing or mediocre record, making them get back to attention to detail with fundamentals is critical. Academics. Position drills. Weight room. Being on time. In everything that they do, they need to dot every i and cross every t. Weed out the lazy.

- In the first few hours or weeks, you will learn more about each of your players by what they do, not by what they say. How did they handle the transition between coaches? Did they skip class, skip workouts, gain weight? Were they leaders? Their body language and attitude will tell you more than their words. Get feedback from staff that has remained in place during the transition: academic counselors, strength coaches, operations staff. Who were our leaders? Who disappeared?

- Teach YOUR way, the best coaches are the ones who are confident enough in their own skin. Repetition, repetition, repetition of your key points, your plan, your mission statement. What is your identity offensively, defensively? What mentality do you want the team to take on? It will take 18-24 months to get things running the way you want them to. Teach, repeat. Teach, repeat.

- If you are taking over a program with a losing or mediocre record, it's okay if you run a few players off. Usually players with bad attitudes and weak work ethics quit or threaten to transfer—let them! These are usually the players who were dead weight, poor leaders and part of the reason that the team was losing in the first place!

> **AS MUCH AS THEY MAY RESIST IT AT FIRST, MOST PLAYERS RESPECT COACHES WHO HOLD THEM TO HIGH EXPECTATIONS.**

- Follow through with what you say you will do, especially with discipline and accountability. Players can see right through coaches when they know they won't be held accountable for their actions and they will quickly lose respect for you. As much as they may resist it at first, most players respect coaches who hold them to high expectations. Don't let your key players get away with a different set of rules, it will come back to bite you.

RECRUITING MADE SIMPLE

- Cut off talk from players about former injustices, favoritism, hardships. When they start in on why they never got a fair shot to showcase their skills, simply tell them that jobs are "wide open" right now!

- Communication is key—be CRYSTAL CLEAR about your rules, expectations and how you want things done. Minimize your goals down to a few points and emphasize, emphasize, emphasize! Be very simple and clear from Day 1.

- Have position coaches meet individually with each player and evaluate their video—immediately! Get a scouting report from your staff and take the time to sit down and meet with each player individually. Be direct and honest with them, look them in the eye. Reiterate your expectations, plan and goals to each one individually. Give them a sheet with rules and expectations in writing—post copies everywhere around the facility!

- Your most important recruits... are already on campus! Understand who you have, and determine what you need! Immediately determine which positions lack depth.

- Always assign responsibilities for coaches who are not out on the road recruiting. Use the time of your staff wisely. If they aren't recruiting, they need to be building player relationships, campus relationships, calling high school coaches, evaluating video, organizing camps, etc. Give everyone specific areas to jump in and manage as you hit the road recruiting.

- Be a strong teacher of the game. Your new players are sizing you up, do you know your stuff? How can you help them win and develop?

- Set up short and long term goals for your team. Communicate these goals and post them so that everyone can see them. 6-week segments, monthly or weekly segments. Start with small goals to get the program back on track.

- Win the campus: develop a list of key university leaders, faculty, Athletic Department staff and student groups that you need to meet with early. Set up a few key meetings to get to know the most important groups or individuals. Write them a hand-written note after the meeting, thanking them for the time and stressing the important role they will play in your program. Be energetic, share your passion about the program enthusiastically!

- Don't diss the old coach to the media, it's not necessary. Instead, promote YOUR plan and staff! Again, it's a waste of time and there is no value in it. Focus on the future not the past, change the storyline.

- Call the parents of your current players to introduce yourself and give them your direct contact information. Get their direct cell phone numbers and emails. Most issues between parents and coaches stem from a lack of communication. Communicate with parents regularly and be sure that they know how to get in touch with you.

- Don't entertain conversations about playing time with parents. Cut them off, tell them that jobs are open and everyone is getting a fair shot. The rest of what they

- have to say in relation to playing time is a waste of your time. Be direct and honest with them about what you are looking for from your players.

- Give key boosters your direct cell number and email- respond to them all. Don't delegate to your assistants or give them generic contact information.

- Hit the ground running with high school coaches. Make a set number of daily calls to high school coaches to introduce yourself. Invite them to practice or clinics. Make sure they feel welcome around your program.

- Develop your Top 25 recruits that you need to be communicating with regularly. Each assistant/position coach needs 25+ players they need to be contacting frequently as well, on top of their broader mailing list of potential prospects.

- Identify your leaders. Whose messages are being heard in the lockerroom, who are a majority of the players following? Are they setting great examples? Do they want to win? Are they making the sacrifices necessary to win? Are they good people? Get them in your office regularly, eat with them in the dining hall, watch film with them.

- Develop key selling points for recruiting. What are the top 3-5 things that make you different, appealing and successful? What are the main reasons that you have drawn your top players to your program? What are your advantages? Use these points in your phone calls, emails, mailouts, social media for recruiting. (See page 128).

- Realize you must make improvements every day – player relations, academics, strength and conditioning, position skills, fundraising, team attitude. Attack the program's weaknesses and strive to have a "win" everyday in the areas that can help you win games. Focus on the core issues and the fundamentals of success.

- What changes to your style of play will you have to make in order for the first season to be successful with the players who are already within the program? Evaluate your personnel. Work with what you have and put your fingerprints on the program over the next 12-18 months. How can you win in the short term while building for the future?

- Keep a daily list of the core areas that need your attention. Laminate it, carry it with you always, put it in your phone, post it around your office and facility. Set alarms in your phone! Follow up with each area daily, assign staff to focus on key areas that need improvement and devote time, energy and resources to fixing the weak points.

- Touch base with recruits who have committed to the former staff. Have you decided to honor their scholarship offer or does your style of play not match up? These prospects will likely speak to the media quickly and it's best to be direct and honest with them on where you are at with evaluations and what is mutually best for you both. Communicate with them directly, don't just avoid them.

RECRUITING MADE SIMPLE

- Even if you are a former player or former coach of that school, you still must get to know the campus, Athletic Department, faculty and staff. Places don't change but the people do, get out and meet the new key people you will be working with.

- Hire a staff that is diverse in strengths, backgrounds, ages. Do not hire a staff that is filled with people just like you. Make a list of strengths your team will need to be successful and put the puzzle together with the coaches and assistants that you bring in.

- Get off on the right foot with the local media. Set up individual meetings with the key beat writers. Be personable. They have a job to do – give them interesting storylines to write about. Help them do their job by providing positive stories, antidotes, humor. Go beyond answering every question with a 'yes' or 'no,' don't give generic responses. Let reporters see your human side. Nothing is ever off the record, so don't say anything that you wouldn't want to read publically!

- Be visible on campus – at the dining hall, at games supporting other university teams, at major student activities, Greek events. You are recruiting students and faculty to attend games and to support your team—get out and shake hands and take selfies! Put weekly effort into this!

- Be yourself.

- In terms of discipline with your players, it's always easier to be tough in the beginning and ease up than to be laid-back and forced to toughen up months later. Set high expectations from Day 1.

- Take time to hire your staff. You are building for the long-term. It's better to hire the right people than just get bodies into the meeting room. Same with recruiting. It's better to get it right than to just get it done fast. Be selective of the people you invite into your program!

- Set dates for a coaching clinic and team camp, communicate these dates with prep coaches in the state and region immediately. Show that building relationships with prep coaches is a top priority to you.

- Get to know your new players personally. Eat meals with them in the dining hall, talk to them about life outside of sports, find out about the important people in their lives and their goals outside of sports. Players will play hard for you when they know you care about them as people. You have to invest that time to get to know them other than their film and stats.

- Get involved in KEY community speaking engagements, you won't be able to say yes to everyone. Your time needs to be limited but any

IF IT DOESN'T HELP YOU SIGN A TOP RECRUIT, LAND A BIG DONATION OR INVOLVE YOUR FAMILY, PUT IT ON HOLD UNTIL AFTER SIGNING DAY! HAVE YOUR ASSISTANT TELL CALLERS AND VISITORS THAT YOU ARE BOOKED UP UNTIL SIGNING DAY.

YOU CAN'T ALLOW YOUR VALUABLE MINUTES (YES, MINUTES!) TO BE WASTED ON NON-URGENT ISSUES, LET ALONE HOURS OR DAYS!

local organization that you can speak to or meet with that helps you sell tickets, energize your fanbase is worth your time. Find out who in the community is the heartbeat of your program – donors, supporters, sponsors, season ticket holders. Energize them and help them draw in more fans!

COVEY'S TIME MANAGEMENT GRID

	URGENT	NOT URGENT
IMPORTANT	QUADRANT I: URGENT & IMPORTANT	QUADRANT II: NOT URGENT & IMPORTANT
NOT IMPORTANT	QUADRANT III: NOT IMPORTANT & URGENT	QUADRANT IV: NOT IMPORTANT & NOT URGENT

SOURCE: Stephen Covey, 7 Habits of Highly Effective People

Quadrant I is for the immediate and important deadlines.
Quadrant II is for long-term strategizing and development.
Quadrant III is for time pressured distractions. They are not really important, but someone wants it now.
Quadrant IV is for those activities that yield little is any value. These are activities that are often used for taking a break from time pressured and important activities.

AS YOUR PHONE IS RINGING OFF THE HOOK AND INVITATIONS ARE ROLLING IN, YOU NEED A VERY SIMPLE SCHEDULE AND YOU NEED TO FOCUS ON THE MOST URGENT AREAS OF THE FOUNDATION OF YOUR PROGRAM!

RECRUITING CYCLE: KEEPING UP WITH LATEST TECHNOLOGY
Another critical aspect of your recruiting operations is staying on top of the latest ways that kids communicate. Undoubtedly, the youth lead these trends. They are (and ALWAYS will be) the first to take over a new app, website or technology in order to express themselves and communicate with each other – oftentimes a full year or more before it takes over mainstream America.

Use these technologies to help push your selling points and visuals out to your prospects in new and fun ways! Post behind-scenes pictures and videos, make your presence known in the newest ways!

Have a member of your staff (preferably one of the youngest or most tech-savvy) stay on top of where "the kids" are today out in cyberspace. They will always be congregating somewhere new—moving far away from where the grown-ups have infiltrated! Staying current with new technologies is an edge in ways to communicate with your prospects and to keep an eye on your current players.

The knowledge you will gain on the recruiting trail and in monitoring your current players (and staying on top of any academic or legal issues) is invaluable. Over the years, I've learned about players getting engaged, having babies, skipping class and losing family members through social media – much faster than waiting for the news to get to the staff. A recruit or player may be having an issue that they aren't telling you about—but they're telling the world about online. Technology can help you understand their psychology or their mood swings! Have a support staffer monitor and make you aware of any major issues.

First Facebook and MySpace. Then Twitter. Then Instagram. Vine. Snapchat. Now Periscope... undoubtedly, it will be somewhere different next week. You must follow where the kids are going. Get ahead on these communication trends before other coaches catch on!

Assign this responsibility to a staff member and make your program, head coach and assistant coaches masters of it, or at least functioning with it.

RECRUITING CYCLE: OFFICIAL & UNOFFICIAL VISIT PLANNING

Official Visits and Unofficial Visits will make or break your program! You will not sign a player if they don't have an enjoyable visit to campus! Period, point blank!

When trying to sell the program on visits, remember that it's just as much about the people as it is about the sport and shiny facilities. Human connection is vital—how would you like the place if you were bringing your own child there on a visit? Put yourself in the shoes of your prospects and their parents. Look at everything from their perspective. You need to maximize the vibe of the visit so it "feels" like it could be a home away from home, don't overlook the smallest of details while planning visits. Simple details or acts sometimes create the greatest connections, and the right connections are what it's all about.

Each Official Visit (and priority Unofficial Visits) need to be customized exactly for your top prospects personally, based on their decision factors. Visits with your priority recruits on campus are not cookie-cutter experiences, they need to be individualized, filled with personal details and unique to each player and their family.

STARBUCKS PHILOSOPHY: THEIR BUSINESS IS JUST AS MUCH ABOUT THE PERSONAL INTERACTIONS AND THEIR ENVIRONMENT AS IT IS ABOUT COFFEE.

Prior to their arrival, send a tentative itinerary to each prospect and their family so they can be prepared of what to expect. Prepare all necessary Compliance and Business Office paperwork. Know names, relationships, contact info and background info (college attended, occupation, marital status) for all guests that are accompanying prospect on the visit. Streamline transportation, know who will be responsible for moving prospects from Point A to Point B (and Point C, Point D,

Point E). Find out what prospects favorite meals are and what they want to see on campus or in the city.

Remember—players often choose programs with their hearts. This is your most critical time to really show what you have to offer—your recruits will likely rule you out or decide to continue on with the process after their Official or Unofficial Visit.

Prospects and their families need to feel heard – that THEIR priorities are YOUR priorities and that their goals can all be achieved at your program. You need a great game plan to show them how each of their decision factors can have a 'yes' checked at your program. Until they feel heard and understood, you cannot influence them. Show them that you're listening and their priorities are important to you, and you will help them achieve each of their goals.

Take their desires and interests into mind and develop a theme that you would like them to walk away from your program thinking. Shape their perception of your program based on their preferences, be sure that they see everything that they want to see, and meet everyone that they want to meet.

Invite them in a personal and detailed way to be an integral part of your program, they need to feel needed and that they can play a key role in your success. Many need to feel like they are the "missing piece" or the catalyst of the Signing Class or position group.

ALWAYS CREATE AN "IT'S AN EXCITING TIME TO BE ON CAMPUS," ATMOSPHERE, AND PROMOTE THE NEW CAMPUS ADDITIONS—NEW BUILDINGS, NEW ATHLETIC FACILITIES, UPGRADES, NEW TECHNOLOGY. EMPHASIZE THAT CAMPUS IS BOOMING AND THEY'LL BE COMING IN AT AN EXCITING TIME!

Little details are just as important as the big ones. Small, genuine gestures can mean more than large, dramatic gestures. Show them that you're listening to their needs and wants.

What is unique and memorable about your program, university and city? What do they need to walk away from remembering?

It is essential that these visits are stress-free, laid-back and enjoyable—they can't see you stressing over transportation logistics or dinner plans—every detail needs to be planned and walked-thru prior to their arrival!

Outdoor activities are a great option while hosting top recruits, especially if climate and backdrop are strong selling points. Be sure to have backup plans for last-minute weather issues, even if the forecast is perfect.

LEAVE NO DETAIL TO CHANCE WHEN IT COMES TO PLANNING OFFICIAL AND UNOFFICIAL VISITS. CUSTOMIZE, PLAN, CONFIRM!

ALWAYS HAVE BACKUP PLANS! EXPECT THE UNEXPECTED:
- Flights are canceled or missed
- Menus change
- Players are delayed because of traffic jams
- Names are not on ticket pass lists
- Long lines are at the prospect pass gates of games
- Recruits show up with unexpected or extra guests

Plan and have a backup plan for as much as you can so that when the prospects and families are in your presence, everything can appear seamless. Have an intern or assistant one step ahead of the group on the itinerary to take care of any issues ahead of time.

After visits with your priority recruits, personally thank them and send a handwritten note to each family. Ask for feedback to find out what they really enjoyed, or if issues of concern came up while on campus.

> **MAJOR CITIES VERSUS SMALL TOWNS:** Recruits are either from small, sleepy towns or major, metropolitan cities. Universities, they're either the heart of a small college town or part of the chaos of major metropolitan cities. Finding a balance between the two are critical when hosting top prospects— big city kids may feel bored in sleepy college towns or small-town players and parents may be easily overwhelmed and intimidated by the big city. You have to find a way to make your environment family-like and a place that won't bore them. Be creative—think of ways you can be flexible and appeal to everyone. You are a small enough community to not be overwhelming, but big enough to not get bored!

RECRUITING CYCLE: CHANGING MINDS

Throughout your career, you will occasionally have great players fall into your lap with little or no work at all—signed, sealed and delivered with no stress. You will also have other players change their mind and sign elsewhere at the last minute after years of recruitment, travel and time invested.

Players are going to change their minds, sometimes at the last minute. Someone close to them may get in their head, for both good and questionable intentions: distance may be a factor, they may be having family issues—you just can never be 100% finished recruiting until the NLI is signed!

But since you are depending on 18-year-olds, making their first big "life" decision, it is part of the job! Undoubtedly, a player that you've built up a great relationship with, and spent a lot of time on, will flip on you and de-commit. It's happened to every coach that I can think of!

The only thing that you can try to do is: do your due diligence during the recruitment process and take the high road after the decision has been made.

In the end, know that it eventually evens out. You may face major frustration one day, then feel like you've hit the lotto the next day. You have to have a "big picture" attitude about your career and treat everyone with respect throughout the process, even if you feel disrespected or heartbroken.

If a top recruit decommits, especially late, you can't overreact. This is a huge decision for these kids, and they have a lot of voices getting into their heads. Some players aren't mature enough to handle recruitment, and fall apart at the end. I've seen it happen to every coach.

In other circumstances, their circle of family and friends may be illegally recruited, and offered impermissible benefits. Family starts heavily pressuring prospects to head in another direction. You always have to keep the big picture in mind, and remember that you need to deal with recruits, families and prep coaches with class. The decision is always out of your hands, you just have to work to put yourself in the best position possible year-round.

You never know, a year or two from now they may be unhappy where they signed and pick up the phone and contact you about transferring. Year after year, I've seen previous recruits change their mind and transfer to play for a coach that they nearly signed with out of high school.

Understand that sometimes the only certainty in recruiting is the uncertainty!

RECRUITING CYCLE: SELF-EVALUATE WITH CURRENT PLAYERS
Each year, sit down with a variety of players from the previous signing class (different backgrounds, rankings, positions, academics, geography) to get a feel for the current recruiting atmosphere. Evaluate your target audience annually, why did your most recent signees choose your program? How did their other visits go? What did they like about their other visits? What type of mail did they receive from other schools? From their standpoint, how can you improve?

RECRUITING CYCLE: PLAYER HOST DECISIONS

Develop a small list of recruiting ambassadors on your roster, players who are the future of your team who are team-oriented and who will be helpful to recruit even more talent to campus.

It's important to put thought into matching hosts with your recruits. Give your hosts a verbal background report on the prospect before their arrival—their wants, their high school, style of play, personality. Match hosts based on personality, position and background to find someone they can relate to on your team. Remember, it's about how a visit feels in terms of the people that helps influence the final decision. Take the time to find a great fit.

WHICH CURRENT PLAYERS WOULD BE GREAT (AND WILLING) AMBASSADORS? WHICH CURRENT PLAYERS WON'T FEEL THREATENED (OR HAVE THEIR ROOMMATE OR BEST FRIEND'S JOB THREATENED).

PERSONALITY TYPES OF RECRUITS:
- Gym Rats
- Religious
- Greek
- Ultra Competitive
- Outgoing
- Home Bodies
- Academic Driven
- Preppy
- Regional Hometowns
- Funny / Easy Going
- Country/Hunters

Invite strength coaches into the discussion, as they spend a lot of time with your players and can provide great insights as to who can be great hosts.

RECRUITING CYCLE: SIGNING DAY

Getting players to commit is the complicated part, but don't forget to have all of your i's dotted and t's crossed for Signing Day. There are still technicalities, like getting the paperwork right! You aren't done until each player is signed, sealed and delivered, and Compliance has signed off!

Send detailed instructions with each packet of scholarship papers. Try to make it as simple and obvious as possible. Since you're dealing with multiple players, streamline the process as simply as you can! Players are excited, stress to them the importance of following your enclosed directions step-by-step. All paperwork needs to be validated, don't drop the ball after the commit!

A week before Signing Day, gather and verify all mailing addresses where paperwork will be sent. If players are under 21 get a feel if there will be any refusal by a parent/guardian to sign off.

After all paperwork is received and validated, and you have the green light from the Athletic Department to publicize, make your announcements personal about each player. This is likely the biggest day of their lives, and up on the list for their parents so give them a big, personalized welcome with cool graphics, bios, social media shoutouts and more!

There will be Signing Day surprises, players who have previously committed who decommit on Signing Day and sign elsewhere. You will lose prospects at the last minute and unfairly, and for reasons you can't control. But, there will be other times in your career when a top recruit will magically land in your lap with little or effort and drama.

RECRUITING CYCLE: PREPARING FOR ENROLLMENT
Shortly after all paperwork is signed, put together lists of academic and admissions deficiencies for each player that need to be taken care of to ensure that enrollment goes smoothly for each signee!

- Academic Needs: Classes to finish with minimum grades needed along with ACT/SAT test scores needed
- Admissions Department Checklist: Transcript info, Applications, Essays, Academic Program Selections, etc.
- Housing Issues: Deposits, dorm selections
- Orientation and Move-in Dates
- Financial Aid
- Class Selection
- Summer School Procedures: Dates, Registration Deadlines, Financial Aid Policies, Housing
- Summer Employment Info

Be sure to send a copy of all key items to parents and guardians as well. Often, important details don't trickle down. Even though recruiting is over, key people still need to be in the loop of mandatory next steps, deadlines and important dates!

CHAPTER #6
RELATIONSHIPS

"There's only one way to succeed in anything, and that is to give it everything. I do, and I demand that my players do."
-VINCE LOMBARDI

"The smallest deed is better than the greatest intention."
-JOHN BURROUGHS

"The greatest leader is not necessarily the one who does the greatest things. He is the one that gets the people to do the greatest things."
-RONALD REAGAN

"Average leaders raise the bar on themselves; good leaders raise the bar for others; great leaders inspire others to raise their own bar."
-ORRIN WOODWARD

RELATIONSHIPS: GET TO KNOW PEOPLE BY NAME

Addressing their customers by name (and by writing it on each overpriced cup of coffee) is an intentional point of emphasis in the Starbucks Customer Service Experience, and likely plays a role in their lucrative customer loyalty. It's no coincidence the billion-dollar brand hand-writes each customers' name on each cup of coffee it sells, it helps build loyalty.

Before we get deep into the topic of building relationships, it's important to stress the importance of getting to know people by name. As a recruiter, you will cross paths with thousands of people each year. You don't have to memorize everyone's name, but if you keep excellent records, you can easily access by phone or in a notebook that you carry with you when out visiting schools or making calls.

New to a school? Taking over a program? Get to know the names of all of your support staff members, interns and student volunteers and address them by name when possible.

From my experiences, there are two types of leaders (and by leader, I mean leadership by position: Athletic Director, Head Coach, Associate AD, Director of Operations)...

#1 – Those who try to demand respect by treating everyone under them exactly as that – by treating everyone as they are if they're below them. When you treat those who are on your 'team' (everyone in your office or building) like they aren't important enough to know their name, they'll perform like their job isn't important. We've all worked with this type of leader before, and rarely are their 'teams' consistently successful.

#2 – Those who earn respect by making everyone on the team want to be the best at their job. Not just the team, but the TEAM behind the TEAM—trainers, student managers, fundraisers, academic counselors, accounting staff, field crew, receptionists, facilities staff, security. Believe it or not, what drives most people to want to be at their best is simple: to feel like what they do makes a difference, and in some way, contributes to the success of the team. People will work harder if they feel that their job or role actually makes a difference. Of the successful teams I've been a part of, the top leadership gets to know the names of everyone on staff.

At the end of the day, most programs have similar resources and selling points to offer outside of win percentages. What separates places from each other are the PEOPLE. Treat your people with respect and recruit great staff and players to go on the adventure with you.

Simply know people's names and greet them when you see them—this gesture will pay dividends for your program in the long run. Think back, at some point we've all been asked to do an over-the-top task or tedious project and thought, "Does this person even know my name?"

ALWAYS SAY, "GREAT TO SEE YOU" INSTEAD OF "NICE MEETING YOU." IF YOU'VE ALREADY MET THE PERSON AND DON'T REMEMBER, IT'S A SLAP IN THE FACE. PLAY IT SAFE WITH A "GREAT TO SEE YOU."

I've worked with 'leaders' who never speak in passing, are too important to know my name and think that this "I'm-above-talking-to-your-pay-grade" attitude makes them instantly credible. It does not. I've learned from some of the best coaches, players and administrators in the business, and most are far from this attitude.

Have Sports Information or a member of your support staff put together a 'cheat sheet' for you, a composite of pictures by department with each person's name and title underneath, with any other details that may help you remember. College or high school attended and hometowns are great ways to associate names and build early connections with these staffers.

Do the same with the reporters who regularly cover your program. Know what paper or station that they work for, and their history with the program (trustworthy, negative, dirty, pot-stirrer). Distribute these lists to all of your coaches—have them memorize all internal staff names as well of people they will deal with on a regular basis.

This gesture will also build accountability within your support staff—nobody is nameless. They will feel more accountable to the program and a part of the organization, and someone you know by name. They will feel more responsibility, more loyalty.

A former boss referred to all of their employees as, "the girl," no matter who they were talking about: their assistant, their intern, the cleaning woman, their next appointment. It's just plain rude, and doesn't help build a feeling of teamwork.

And, stop calling every prep coach "Coach." You need to know prep coaches by their last name. As you don't like when prospects send you form letters and refer to you as a coach at your rival school, prep coaches expect the same respect and address them as "Coach _____." Keep excellent records so you can reference coaches names at your fingertips.

It may sound very silly to have to tell you this, even about your own staff, but I've seen it happen too many times, and it never brings great results.

YOUR STAFF SEEKS ACKNOWLEDGEMENT AND APPRECIATION, NOTHING WILL GO FURTHER THAN A SINCERE PAT ON THE BACK OR PUBLIC SHOUTOUT. BUILD AN ORGANIZATION WHERE YOU ENTIRE STAFF IS DRIVEN AND FEELS PART OF YOUR SUCCESS.

RELATIONSHIPS: YOUR OWN FAMILY

You could spend every minute of your day on recruiting and still not have enough time. As you are building a career, also remember to build a life!

As you budget your time and earn to say no to requests that aren't important, be sure to schedule quality time with your family: your parents, your spouse and your children. Quality time can make up for quantity of time in terms of family time. Coaches kids and spouses are usually used to the lifestyle, but there are ways to improve the limited time you feel you have with your family. They're making sacrifices for you and your career, find small gestures or family rituals that show you care and can be active in their lives too.

- Be present when you're having family time. Date night is not date night if you are on the phone half the time (or more)!

- Find pockets of time each week that you can work in family time: a day you can get home early, a morning you can take the kids to school yourself, a family dinner at a campus restaurant, evenings when your kids can come to the end of practice, a lunch date with your spouse, a pre-game or post-game tradition.

- Cut your commute down and live close to campus. Be more accessible to home so they can visit you more often or you can sneak home to tuck the kids into bed or eat dinner together.

- If you are able to, take your kids with you on local evaluation trips. Let them see what you do.

- Try to spend individual time with each child occasionally. An ice cream run, a Sunday breakfast, a quick shopping trip to the mall for a good report card. Children value one-on-one time and attention!

- Show genuine interest in your spouse's day. A simple, uninterrupted 10-minute conversation, starting with "How was your day?" can do wonders for a marriage. Sympathize with their daily load, they are putting in more household work than the average marriage.

- Go home when you can. There will always be a week or two here and there when you can get out of the office early, make calls or watch video from home after the kids go to bed. You can't stay cooped up in your office.

- Although the last thing you probably want to do in your off time is travel, a mini-vacation (or staycation) is a great way to spend quality time with your spouse and kids. Schedule an overnight out of town or nearby every month or two.

- Encourage your children's hobbies (and spouse) and take an active interest in their progress and participation.

> **QUALITY TIME CAN MAKE UP FOR QUANTITY OF TIME IN TERMS OF FAMILY TIME.**

RELATIONSHIPS: PROGRAM LEADERS

As a coach, realize that PEOPLE are your greatest resource. A priority each offseason is to identify your leaders for the next season. Teams change drastically every year. Players graduate, transfer in, transfer out, quit, get injured... and more importantly, GROW UP at their own pace. Your strengths and weaknesses as a team will change from year-to-year. Always have a pulse on whose influence is being heard in the lockerroom and huddle.

- Your leaders will determine the success of your team. If nobody steps up in the lockerroom, the huddle or practice, your team will fall flat in game situations. Put time into leadership development for all players, especially your starts or 2-deep.

- Leaders create other leaders. There is a ripple effect, a domino effect, a reverse peer-pressure effect. Ask yourself, "Who is at the head of this thing?" Whose messages are being heard, which players have the most influence on their teammates? Are they using it positively?

- Your leaders won't always be starters, seniors or scholarship players. Some of the greatest leaders I've worked with were walk-ons, back-ups and even freshmen! Oftentimes, you will have players with great attitudes and work ethics in this less-skilled group. Their leadership can contribute to the success of your team just as much as your star players. Recognize and acknowledge their efforts and attitudes!

- Not all seniors, starters or scholarship players are capable of leadership. Not everyone has "it" when it comes to leadership.

- Some players are faux-leaders. Starters or upperclassmen—who have a voice and whose messages are heard—who can be destructive to your team. Players who complain about everything. They're never at fault. They don't take responsibility. They always have an excuse. They're always placing blame. They're the biggest threat to your offseason. They can also be reformed... by the leaders of ACTION. Identify them and work with them individually to change their ways. Find out what else is going on in their life that can be causing the negativity.

- Ask your assistant coaches, your strength coaches, your managers, your academic staff, your trainers: "Who are our leaders?" Many players carry themselves differently throughout the facility and act different with other members of the staff. Some players act different when the head coach or their position coach isn't around.

- Identify your leaders as a staff. Publicly praise them. Point out what they're doing right, acknowledge their actions that will translate to success for your program. Point out what they do right in front of the rest of the team. Give them more responsibility. Expect even more greatness from them. Encourage them to create other leaders. These efforts can translate to the difference that you will need to win close games.

Never forget that PEOPLE are your greatest resource. Identify your best ones immediately and develop as many other potential leaders that you can! You need more than X's and O's to win big and win consistently!

RELATIONSHIPS: YOUR CURRENT PLAYERS

To get the most out of your players, to push them beyond where they think they can go athletically, you must continue to develop this relationship consistently. And to sign great players for tomorrow, you must do an excellent job with the players you have now! You must continuously "recruit" your players, even after they've enrolled.

When done the right way, 20 years later, players look back at their coaches as parent figures, a mentor who played an influential role in their development as a person, not just a player. From 18-years-old to graduation into adulthood, you are involved in their lives during a key time. You are in the trenches together, missing holidays and family events together, working together, overcoming adversities together, competing at a high level together... these are some of the strongest bonds you can build outside of your family. Experiencing the highest of highs—WINNING—and the lowest of lows—LOSING—bonds you! Few outside of the walls of your team meeting room really understand the struggle and sacrifices that you're all making.

Very few other "careers" have this dynamic. Coaching isn't just a job or career, it's a lifestyle. You get the reward of watching players grow up, when the light comes on and to know them as they finally mature into adults!

- Be proactive in your approach with your players. Check up on them as if they were your own kids. Call them, text them, find them on social media. Be in their lives outside of the meeting room and practice. Even in the offseason, you should be speaking with your players on a weekly basis. Check in on grades, life situations, family and how they're doing spiritually.

- You need to have the cell phone numbers of your players as well as their class schedules and current email address. Shoot them a text when their favorite team or pro player is playing. Check in with them while you're out recruiting. Know them outside of sports, play a consistent, dependable role in their life.

- Don't be so buttoned up and intimidating that your players can't express themselves with you, or that you can't express your genuine pride in them. You want to remain respected, and not necessarily their buddy, but let your guard down enough to develop a real genuine relationship. Eat together in the dining hall or food court, invite them to your house occasionally for a meal (with approval from Compliance Office), have your family and your position group interact together, eventually as family. Make decisions impacting your players as if they were your own kids. As they eventually feel part of your family, that's just one extra layer of accountability and responsibility they'll feel – players live up to the expectations they're held to.

- Over the years I've learned that 99% of players respond to expectations—not yelling. Expect greatness and perfection (or near perfection) from your players, teach them the way, and give them the tools to succeed. Yelling doesn't usually work, expectations do!

- Be crystal clear with team rules and policies and hold all players to the same rules and standards. Team chemistry is disrupted and relationships weaken when rules don't apply to certain players. Once you start making exceptions and letting key players get away with more rule-breaking, it's the beginning of the end for you in that lockerroom.

- Recognize and applaud players that are doing it the right way, players that buy in and are exceeding expectations throughout every area of life.

> **ONCE YOU START MAKING EXCEPTIONS AND LETTING KEY PLAYERS GET AWAY WITH MORE RULE-BREAKING, IT'S THE BEGINNING OF THE END FOR YOU IN THAT LOCKERROOM.**

RELATIONSHIPS: FAMILIES OF CURRENT PLAYERS

Just because you've already signed their kids, that doesn't mean that you can stop recruiting them to be a part of the program as well. The main issue that I've heard over the years from parents is the lack of communication directly TO parents. Information about important dates, schedules and events doesn't always trickle down from the player to their parent, so it's greatly appreciated if you communicate these details to them directly.

Parents love feeling included – keep an email database, a mailing list, a text list... whatever works for your program, or all three. Find the best way to communicate with your parents and communicate regularly! Continue to communicate just as regularly as you did when you were recruiting their kids!

Over the years, parents of your current and former players will grow into a large network – a group that can help or hurt you later in your career. Remember—parents talk, and a lot of athletes are connected. The relationship that you have with your players and their families, and how they're treated under your leadership, is one of the best references you can have. Good or bad, parents will talk frankly, especially if asked for their opinion!

RELATIONSHIPS: COMMITS

No matter how solid their commitment may seem, never slack off on your efforts towards a player who has already committed to your program. Getting them to say "yes" is only part of the job, keeping them locked up, excited and interested in your program is still your responsibility.

If you begin taking your committed prospects for granted, knowing you've got them locked up, and start focusing all of your attention on the next great targets (that you are under pressure to secure), a rival coach can sneak up and steal them out from under you. Rival coaches may continue conversations with Mom, continue to show up at their games and prove to the athlete that they're more wanted at their schools. Rival coaches can still try to convince them that they would make more of an impact at their program than yours. Many rival coaches don't stop recruiting even if a player has committed, depending on the sport. You must continue to recruit your committed players just as heavily as your top uncommitted players, if not even harder.

In many cases, top prospects still don't know how to handle the whole process: interacting in adult conversations, feeling torn between their wants and their parents and friends opinions. A lot of recruits are afraid to say the wrong thing or are uncomfortable discussing other schools with you—always remember this is likely the biggest decision or stressor they've faced so far in life.

Between college coaches putting pressure on them to commit, social media noise, listening to 50 opinions from friends and family, media speculation, message board rumors—prospects can be under a lot of pressure. Many can be swayed week-to-week to change their mind. Once a player commits, the sharks really come out! Keep recruiting and keep communicating!

RELATIONSHIPS: RECRUITS WITH SPECIAL NEEDS
Assigning recruiting coaches can't always be done in a cookie-cutter format – just because a particular player falls into a geographic region or position – always remember the personal side of relationship-building is most important.

Maybe a player is going through a death or sickness of a parent, maybe another assistant who has experienced a similar heartbreak would be a better recruiter. Maybe they're transferring, extremely interested in a particular major or are of a certain religion, have children or a spouse, play multiple sports, have a learning disability. Have your staff detail their backgrounds and life story to determine their strengths in building relationships.

For your top recruits – evaluate the "fit" and ability to develop a natural relationship with the assigned regional recruiting coach. Some people just don't mesh well, would another assistant be a better contact? As a staff, have a system to evaluate and re-assign key prospects if necessary.

RELATIONSHIPS: PARENTS OF RECRUITS
Before you even make your first call, always keep in mind that Mom and Dad often hold the veto card. As this is the first major decision most players are making-- no matter how independent or tough they seem – recruits often go to their parents for approval and advice before making their final decision.

Too many times, I've seen a "best on paper" opportunity for the prospect, and their interest and desire in a program ultimately be vetoed by Mom or Dad. The school is too far away, there's not enough early playing time, it's in too big of a city, it's not an academically prestigious university... for whatever the reason (true or not), Mom and Dad often have the veto power to eliminate schools.

UNDERSTAND THAT PARENTS, MORE OFTEN, HAVE THE POWER TO SAY NO AND ELIMINATE A SCHOOL THAN TO SAY YES AND MAKE THE DECISION.

While winning over the parents can definitely help your cause, it's important to also evaluate if you think the parents will sabotage the decision in the end. Many prospects will drop a school if Mom or Dad doesn't approve, and sometimes they wait until the end of the process to do so when their parents finally put their foot down. If a parent is dead set against them signing with you from the start (usually too far from home or not academically prestigious enough), you need to decide how much time you want to invest in their recruitment. It's over before it even gets started in some cases.

While you will need to win both parents over, you especially need to make a friend in Mom. Mom will be asking questions, doing her homework and putting you through the ringer before handing over her baby! No matter how old the prospect is, to Mom-- she's undoubtedly going to do her homework on you and your university. You need to be informative and personable with Mom, have the answers to her questions before she even asks and build her trust! She's sizing you up as a parent away from home, not necessarily just an X's and O's coach. She's not evaluating only what you can do for her child during games, she's looking all phases of her child's life on your campus.

You need to envision the "family away from home" situation that you will be providing when coming up with your recruitment plan for parents. Put yourself in their shoes, they're putting their greatest possession in life in your hands. You will be the mentors that will help their child transition into adulthood. Tailor your recruiting pitch to parents differently than how you sell the program to recruits-- and each family will be different. What values are important to you and upheld within your program?

SURE... WINS, GEAR, DRAFT SUCCESS, TV GAMES AND EARLY PLAYING TIME ARE FUN AND EXCITING BUT A MAJORITY OF PARENTS ONLY REALLY CARE ABOUT "LIFE AFTER SPORTS," THEIR EDUCATION AND THEIR LIFE EXPERIENCE OPPORTUNITIES ON CAMPUS. THIS IS WHERE YOU CAN SEPARATE YOURSELF AS A RECRUITER!

When selling the program to most parents, lead with academics! At the end of the day, most parents focus a lot of attention on academics-- always have an academic mention in your talks and notes. If the player isn't a great student, promote ability to help the player with tutors, technology, internships and track records with former player academic improvements. (See page 121 for more advice on recruiting parents.)

ACADEMIC CONVERSATION TOPICS FOR PARENTS:
- Academic Advising
- Job Fairs
- Academic Progress Rates
- Graduation Success Rates
- Internship Opportunities
- Majors
- Career Development
- Job Placement
- Cost of Degree
- Graduation Pictures
- Companies That Hire Recent Graduates
- Small Class Size
- University Academic Program Rankings
- Online Campus Tours
- Campus Pictures
- Campus Leadership
- Team GPA
- Quotes from Former Players about Their Academic Experience
- Campus Speakers
- Student-Athletes in Leadership Roles on Campus
- Student-to-Faculty Ratios
- University Admission Rates (if selective)

A key complaint that I've heard over the years is that parents aren't always informed by their children, so you need to share key information with them directly as well, because it won't always trickle down to them. Important conversations also need to be brought up with parents, get to know their likes and dislikes. Ask them if they have questions about what to expect, and if they want some advice on what to expect. Help them eliminate stress and anxiety about the process with a general conversation about the process. Share updates about your program with them, dates of upcoming events so that they can plan, and congratulations on their children's accomplishments! You need to build a direct relationship with parents as well.

WHILE YOU WANT TO EMPHASIZE YOUR PRIORITY OF GRADUATION AND ACADEMICS, YOU DON'T WANT TO OVERWHELM WEAK STUDENTS AND TURN THEM OFF. EACH PITCH WILL BE DIFFERENT DEPENDING ON EACH STUDENT AND FAMILY.

AFTER GREAT CONVERSATIONS OR VISITS, DROP A HANDWRITTEN NOTE OR LETTER IN THE MAIL TO PARENTS THANKING THEM FOR THEIR TIME, COMPLIMENTING THEIR CHILD'S SKILLS OR INTANGIBLE STRENGTHS, THEIR ROLE AS A PARENT. BE GENUINE AND THANKFUL, YOU DON'T HAVE TO ALWAYS BE "SELLING."

What matters most to the parents of your top prospects needs to matter to you, they want to be heard and understood (as long as it's within the rules and your program's philosophy). What values or decision factors are important to each prospect's family?

When dealing with parents, always remember that you are building a career and that parents all talk to each other. Never promise something that you can't deliver, or have no intention of ever delivering. You will run into uncomfortable situations, there will be times when you have to give bad news to parents. In all situations with prospects and their families, it's best to be honest and direct with them. Don't lead prospects and their families on a wild goose hunt. Don't continuously dodge their calls or just fall out of communication with them. Parents and prep coaches talk and share information on character and integrity, respect carries on for decades.

MORE PARENT TIPS:
- Always consider this: you will be linked to the parents and families of your signees for the next few years. Their attitudes will be magnified once their child is enrolled. Supportive parents become great assets, and difficult parents become even more of a disability and nuisance. Keep this in mind as you move forward-- parents will always be in their child's ear. They will either be promoting a good attitude and work ethic through tough times (which all players go through), or they'll be a negative force, stirring the pot and creating extra drama when you need it least. Again, parents can help you or hurt you so proceed with caution and consider this during recruiting!

- On the topic of playing time with parents: never let parents dictate how you do your job. Of the most successful coaches that I've worked with, parents calling about playing time has resulted in the player remaining on the bench. Parents who badger you about playing time during the recruiting process will only scream louder once their child is enrolled and plant negative seeds in the player's mind. During the recruiting process, offer players an opportunity to "compete"-- not necessarily a guaranteed starting job.

- An unwritten rule in recruiting: head coaches are looking to hire married coaches. A married assistant coach is perceived much more trustworthy and reliable while a single coach is perceived as a bachelor or bachelorette. True or not, many head coaches prefer to fill their staff with a majority of married assistant coaches.

- If you are married, invite your spouse to be able to be a part of important visits, especially events that parents attend. When creating a "family" atmosphere, get as many family members that you think would be good ambassadors to recruiting events. Great recruiters often have spouses who are also great recruiters– friendly, knowledgeable, supportive and great closers. Talk to your head coach about possibly including spouses during select recruiting events, Official Visits or Unofficial Visits. Check with the Business Office and Compliance Office about restrictions.

RELATIONSHIPS: PREP COACHES

Simply put– your network and relationships with prep coaches will #1- be the key to signing recruits and #2- be the key to getting future jobs.

YOU WILL BE SPEAKING TO PREP COACHES AS MUCH AS, IF NOT MORE THAN, RECRUITS.

The best philosophy is this: you need to treat every prep coach as if they have a top prospect on their team now. You are recruiting for the long-term and building your career, and there is a good chance that one year, five years, 10 years from now... a no-name coach at an unsuccessful school may have a great player for you! A prep coach may go from an unheard of program to a traditional powerhouse program down the road. If you make a bad impression on a prep coach when they have nothing to help you, they'll remember. The best recruiters implement this philosophy early in their careers and build every relationship possible.

You need to invest time each day building and strengthening relationships with prep coaches. EVERY DAY. Prep coaches are the gatekeepers who can help or hurt your cause. You will need to go through them to get prospect phone numbers, access to prospects and to pass mail or initial interest along, especially early in the process. You also will want strong relationships so that prep coaches will trust and respect you, and pick up the phone to call you and tip you off about great young prospects.

A strategy to help you long-term: pick a region of the country and prioritize building a great reputation in that area, building strong relationships throughout. Assistant coaches are often hired because of their "pipeline" to a specific region. If you really focus on building great relationships in a specific area, it can help you get jobs in the future– especially if it is considered a "hotbed" area with several prospects each year.

It's easy to get wrapped up in your daily responsibilities but if you take a second to Google what's going on in their world before you make a call, you show that you've been doing your research on them. You can quickly reference their upcoming schedule and already know who they're playing or who they just beat. Saying "Congrats on that big win over Northeast" sounds a lot better than, "So... who did ya'll play last week?" Congratulate them on wins, wish them good luck on upcoming games, give them shoutouts on achievements– take that extra step to know a detail of what's going on with them before you call. Separate yourself among all the other college coaches that are also reaching out to them.

All dealings with prep coaches need to be positive, prep coaches need to feel as if you're doing everything possible to help them. Show genuine interest in them and their program. Many of them are former players, they need to feel invited and wanted around your program. You need to have an "open door" policy for prep coaches, invite and welcome them into your program. In order for trust and a relationship to grow, people need to feel heard. Take the time to listen to your prep coaches and devote time to hearing them out.

THE BEST PHILOSOPHY IS THIS: YOU NEED TO TREAT EVERY PREP COACH AS IF THEY HAVE A TOP PROSPECT ON THEIR TEAM NOW.

Quickly return voicemails and emails when possible– even if you're sure it's a dead end. Send a coded questionnaire out as a good gesture showing that you are following through on the lead. Take two minutes to make a return call, even if you are "stepping into a team meeting," and especially if it's a program within the state or city.

Great recruiters manage their time in order to maximize their ability to call as many prep coaches that they can, daily. Great recruiters make back-to-back-to-back-to-back-to-back-to-back-to-back-to-back-to-back-to-back-to-back-to-back-to-back calls to prep coaches. Checking in, getting schedules, asking about up-and-coming players, congratulating them on wins or achievements, inviting them to camps or Unofficial Visits or just shooting the breeze. If you expect high school coaches to help you and return calls, you need to help them and be responsive to their calls and emails too.

With all your responsibilities, time management with prep coaches will be a difference-maker for you. While you need to treat all prep coaches as if they're a high priority, you need to master the art of getting in and out of conversations quickly and genuinely. Make a quick call before a practice, meeting or flight... "Coach, we're about to step into a staff meeting (practice, team meeting, compliance meeting), just wanted to give you a quick call back."

CENTER CONVERSATIONS WITH PREP COACHES ON WHAT IS GOING ON IN THEIR WORLD, NOT PATTING YOURSELF ON THE BACK OF ALL YOUR ACCOMPLISHMENTS AND RESPONSIBILITIES.

You need to reach out to the former prep coaches of your current players, throughout the year. Just because you already signed their player, that doesn't mean recruitment has ended. You still need to keep in touch, and if financially possible, always include them in recruit mailouts.

Although difficult at times, it's always best to be up front and honest (with tact) with prep coaches about their prospects if they're not going to make the cut. After seeing them play, if you have no interest in their player, it's best to be honest with them. Always be open and willing to "take a look," but don't lead anyone on with false hope. Give them a few pointers of what improvements they would need to make in order to be legitimately considered, characteristics that the prospect can actually improve on or control. You will quickly damage your reputation and lose respect when you begin jerking prep players and coaches around. Remember-- you are building a career and will likely cross paths with these coaches years from now.

"A WINNER MAKES COMMITMENTS. A LOSER MAKES PROMISES."

Another great way to help build relationships with prep coaches is to be a teaching resource for them. They will likely ask for sample drills, schemes or gameplanning advice– have a few email-ready files ready to share. Be a mentor and be a resource to those younger or less experienced coaches wanting to learn more.

Extra Credit: Drop a quick handwritten note in the mail after a conversation with a prep coach (or any key gatekeeper). A couple handwritten sentences and a stamp can go a long way in the world of texts, tweets and RTs. You can even pre-write or have your assistant handle.

WHAT TO TALK ABOUT:
- Upcoming schedules.
- Invite them to practice or games.
- Player recommendations (underclassmen, other players in area).
- Ask how your prospects are doing in school, at practice, in games and mentally.
- Talk shop: Philosophy, teaching drills, rule changes, current news with your sport, pros in your sport, other sports.
- Ask them for feedback about your program: their perception, what they think of your head coach, your style of play.

BE RESPECTFUL:
- Ask when the best time to call is, which days and times work best?
- When planning visits, ask what time works for them and try to plan your visit around their schedule.
- If running late for an appointment or visit, call and let them know. Give them an estimated time of arrival and your cell phone number.
- Send a handwritten thank you note after great conversations or visits. Have pre-stamped notes with you to carry on the road or send immediately when back in the office.
- Keep them involved and updated in the recruiting process when actively recruiting one of their players.
- Write a letter to their principal or supervisor, thanking or applauding them for their efforts, attitude or leadership.
- Never make a promise to a prep coach that you can't deliver on. They'll know that your words can't be trusted, and they won't appreciate you leading their players on.

WAYS TO HELP:
• Pass along drills or offensive/defensive tips if coaches ask. Be a teaching resource.
• Invite successful and up-and-coming coaches to work camps. Use that time to build relationships with them on campus socially- eat together, talk shop, get to know about their goals and family.
• If you aren't interested in a player that they're pitching and know a coach at a lower division who probably would be, offer to recommend the player to another collegiate coach on their behalf.

Types of Mail:
• **Motivational:** They are under the same schedules as you. Send them occasional "We know what you're going through..." notes or great quotes they can use for their players.
• **Informative:** Major program or university points (program, academics) as well as sport knowledge (offensive/defensive drills, philosophy.)
• **Events:** Practice, Games, Clinics, Junior Days, Camps.
• **Congrats:** Team Rankings (National, State), Coach of an All-State teams/player. You need to notice and recognize their achievements!

RELATIONSHIPS: HIGH SCHOOL STAFFERS

A secret weapon that great recruiters recognize are the non-coaching staffers at high schools. Administrative assistants, guidance counselors, school security guards, janitors, principals, assistant principals... staffers that interact with student-athletes are great contacts for you to develop, in addition to prep coaches. And many of these contacts carry over year-to-year, so as you look to build your career, these contacts can help you every year when you come back, particularly for schools that you look to build a pipeline in.

Administrative assistants in any office are the eyes and ears that can be great resources for you-- they see and hear everything. From the top to the bottom, they are goldmine of information-- and they are gatekeepers that can help you get through to a variety of contacts, and can help you get things done, especially if a coach or guidance counselor isn't very responsive or helpful. They can help get you a transcript, phone number, schedule, signature.

In all your dealings at high schools-- never underestimate the support staff on the ground, you have to work beyond the coaching staff. You will likely have bumps in the road collecting everything through the process at each school, these long-tenured staffers can help you get things done when coaches won't!

Prep coaches aren't always your only (or best) source of information, especially if they have allegiances to coaches at other colleges or programs. Prep athletes interact with a variety of staffers outside of coaches, don't overlook anyone. Always carry yourself in a friendly and approachable manner, especially at in-state programs.

Remember names of assistants, get their direct contact info during your dealings on campus or on the phone, be friendly-- these are also key contacts you need to recruit! When calling or stopping by, ask or speak to them by name. If you are organized in your note-taking, this will be an easy bonus connection for you.

RELATIONSHIPS: ASSISTANT COACHES ON YOUR STAFF

A trust test of a great head coach is not only their ability to put together a great coaching staff, but to manage one that can work together effectively. Whether you are a head coach or an assistant coach, you will be dealing with staff issues.

As you preach to your players the value of teamwork and expecting them to have an unselfish mentality, a lot of coaches forget these expectations in the staff meeting room. Understandably – coaching is an ultra-competitive business with the potential for huge pay days, and most coaches are striving for their next promotion. Coaches are naturally looking to crush the competition and that attitude is sometimes hard to turn off within the walls of your own staff meeting room.

It's unrealistic to expect the entire staff to be best friends – but it is realistic for coaches to carry themselves professionally within their own facility walls. How do you expect your team to get better when the coordinators are always taking shots at each other, if position coaches are questioning each other in front of the team or if particular coaches claim all of the responsibility for successes in certain areas?

WHAT SEPERATES GREAT STAFFS FROM AVERAGE STAFFS:

- **TRUST**: Head coaches should hire great assistants, preferably ones they've had a history or relationship with, and trust them to do their job, with results being evaluated annually. There are several layers within each program that need daily attention, so delegation must be trusted! Successful organizations empower their members to make decisions, based off of a standard set of values or rules, increasing productivity and efficiency. Realistically, there will be disagreements, egos, competition, politics and tense times. A lot is on the line: families, careers, houses, promotions, media pressure. How you handle disagreements, and how your staff handles disagreements will impact the success of your team.

- **UNSELFISHNESS**: As you preach to your players: "There is enough shine out there for everyone." You don't need one superstar player, you need a whole roster full of great players who can contribute value. Same with coaching staffs – there are PLENTY of responsibilities that you can prove your value with, and ways to boost your resume. Find a niche within the program where you can make your mark!

- **WINNING**: Your job will be judged on the success of your position group and your ability to recruit. As a staff, you'll likely be judged solely on winning. The greatest staffs focus on winning, what it takes to win, finding an edge to help them win, ways to win in recruiting, helping their players develop into winners. Everything else is irrelevant if your staff can't win as a whole. Everyone will be out of a job.

- **MONEY ISSUES**: Issues with your paycheck are between you and the head coach and Athletic Director or Assistant AD overseeing your sport. If another assistant is making more, remember that's the salary you agreed to. Keep money talks strictly between you and your direct supervisor. Money talks are extremely destructive among staffs. Renegotiate your contract or find another job. If you are a head coach, are you able to provide financial incentives for exceeding goals or able to assign new responsibilities to your top assistants looking for promotions or more responsibility? You need to plan ahead in order to keep great assistants growing and improving within your program, and that includes some financial incentive.

- **LEADERSHIP**: Stick to the head coach's mission statement and team goals – communicate these standard goals enthusiastically and often. Keep everyone focused on the tasks at hand, not focused on the dynamics of personalities between the staff. Keep your energy positive, walk away from the negativity. Diffuse petty situations.

- **CONTRIUBTION**: Take an active role in meetings! Contribute ideas, don't be afraid to speak up. Don't be too sensitive if your ideas are shot down or not implemented, there are often outside reasons. Continue to generate ideas.

- **SET EXAMPLE**: You cannot carry yourself with a, "Do as I say, not as I do," attitude and expect your players to be accountable. You must lead with the same behaviors that you expect of them.

- **RESPECT**: Never talk negativity about other coaches or staff in front of players. They will mirror you. In front of players or other staffers, always refer to coaches as "Coach _____" or call them by their first name. Never call other coaches by a nickname or by their last name in front of players, set the expectation of respect.

- **NO GOSSIP**: Zero tolerance on gossip among staff and spouses, it's counterproductive to your team's mission. If it's an issue, limit what you share with your spouse. You don't want to create tension between coach's spouses or families. Come to work to do your job. Focus your time on handling your responsibilities and making your areas of the program successful and strengths of the team. You should have more than enough to do!

RELATIONSHIPS: ATHLETIC DEPARTMENT

As you move up throughout your career you will need allies in the front office, not just in coaching circles. If you eventually aspire to be a head coach– next year or 10 years from now– you need to invest some time building relationships with the Assistant ADs in the Athletic Department, and make a good impression with the Athletic Director.

Just as you aspire to be a head coach, these up-and-coming future Athletic Directors are also putting together their career plans and one day may have the power to hire you, or influence someone else in their circle to hire you. If you're a grad assistant or assistant coach, look around at your peers within the Athletic Department, all the other interns and entry- level staffers also aspire to run the show one day too! Build careers together.

You need to build your network among coaches, yes, but also with these current and future decision-makers who can hire you or get your resume on top of the pile with Athletic Directors. Other coaches have the power to hire you as an assistant coach, but Athletic Directors have the power to hire you as a Head Coach. Get them and future Athletic Directors in your circle early!

RECRUITING MADE SIMPLE

A pet peeve among Athletic Department staffers is feeling that they are being treated unprofessionally or in an unorganized way. Recruiting involves lots of paperwork, approvals and assistance from several other internal departments and involvement during Official/Unofficial Visits. You must be organized with them and not constantly overstress their jobs because of lack of preparation on your part.

It's a good idea to sit down with staffers within the Athletic Department, and throughout the University, people who you will deal with on a regular basis. Give them advance notice on what is coming up, come up with a plan together of what you need to work together successfully. Don't be caught off-guard at the last minute with paperwork requirements and approval processes, it quickly irritates everyone around the department and you'll develop a reputation of being rude or unorganized.

Depending on your off-field responsibilities, you may have to interact and have some difficult dealings with administrators regarding budget, player discipline, compliance, staffing or politics. Try to always keep these tough conversations professional, you can have conflicting opinions or stances in these areas, but always look for the best and most professional ways to resolve them.

I've worked with some coaches who take on a "me-versus-the-world" attitude when dealing with others staffers in the Athletic Department, and others who look to network with everyone department-wide. Guess which ones have had more successful careers? You need as much help for your program that you can get, and remember that you are building a reputation within the Athletic Department, and word spreads nationally.

Always assume that anyone in the Athletic Department can eventually help you, whether it's getting a job or through recruiting relationships. You never know who will help you down the road. With the high rate of turnover in Athletic Departments, your network and contacts at other schools will quickly multiply as everyone moves up and takes jobs at other schools.

Along with administrators, be cordial and appreciative with other departments—Marketing, Ticket Office, Training Room. For your team, these staffers will work harder for you and be ambassadors for your program if you make them feel like they are a valuable PART of the program.

At monthly or quarterly all-staff department meetings or Athletic Department social events, be sure to get out of your shell and away from your day-to-day established contacts and sit with some new people that you don't know yet, or contacts you haven't spent much face-to-face time with. Build friendships outside of your sport. Be friendly and approachable.

And yes, while this is their job, many staffers will go above and beyond for your program. There will be a last-minute request or big favor you'll need one day, start off on the right foot. Make sure you take the time to thank them after big recruiting weekends – send a personal note, pick up the phone and ask for feedback on how to make improvements in procedures. Annually, plan a lunch or dinner to thank those who consistently help you throughout the year. Make them feel like an appreciated and necessary part of your program.

EXTEND APPRECIATION: REWARD THOSE WITHIN ATHLETIC DEPARTMENT
- Walk around Athletic Department and give away extra camp t-shirts (after camp) or marketing giveaway items for upcoming or recent games.
- Offer a camp discount to department staff's children (with Compliance's approval, for children under a recruitable age).
- Pick up the phone and leave a quick voicemail to shoutout other teams, coaches and staff on their big wins, upcoming games or awards.
- Invite other young staffers to lunch on campus, build relationships that make sense.
- Start a mentorship panel and get together for lunch or dinner monthly
- Organize department social events- BBQs, bowling, trivia nights, kickball leagues.
- Ask older, more experienced staffers for career advice. Ask just a few questions, and sit back and listen. Let them do most of the talking.
- Write personal thank you notes– a lost art that is still impactful!
- Pick up some donuts or Starbucks and deliver them personally for extra assistance or hard work!
- Invite key staffers to a team meal or team function, if approved by head coach and allowable by budget.
- Attend games of other sports teams and post your support on social media!
- Work out in the communal staff gym. Many staffers get a workout in the early morning or at lunch.
- Thank supportive staff or departments publically for their assistance and give them a social media shoutout, especially on Signing Day, Graduation, Registration, End of Season, etc.
- Organize a Field Day for staff: softball game or friendly competition.
- Give extra gear or t-shirts to children of staff members.

RELATIONSHIPS: YOUR OFFICE STAFF
Sure, you're busting your butt, working long hours and spending time away from family. A way to be even more efficient and productive– have a great support staff of grad assistants, operations staff, administrative assistants and interns.

If you hire people who are capable and excited about your program– maximize their impact by appreciating them. Give them a steady responsibility, something they can take ownership of... something that makes them feel as if they make a difference (see page 178). If you trust them, train and delegate something interesting to them to be an impactful part of "the team," not just handing down busy work.

Your staff are gatekeepers – they can do a good job or a lousy job of turning around your reimbursements, screening calls, keeping unsolicited time-wasters out of your office, giving you tips on office gossip or what they're hearing from players– these staffers are usually the eyes and ears of the office and know what's going on when you're not around.

A little bit of appreciation goes a long way with this group. Many of these positions are underpaid and underappreciated, but can be a secret weapon for you. You can get a lot of help from the right person, or they can be dead weight, depending on who you hire and how you train and treat them. Five minutes of your time each day-- a simple chat while you open your mail and ask how their day is, how their family is doing, or an occasional Starbucks or lunch out goes a long way.

> **WHAT DRIVES MOST PEOPLE TO WANT TO BE AT THEIR BEST IS SIMPLE: TO FEEL LIKE WHAT THEY DO MAKES A DIFFERENCE, AND IN SOME WAY CONTRIBUTES TO THE SUCCESS OF THE TEAM. PEOPLE WILL WORK HARDER FOR YOU IF THEY FEEL THAT THEIR JOB OR ROLE ACTUALLY MAKES A DIFFERENCE. EVERYONE WANTS A PURPOSE AND A RESPONSIBILITY!**

The good thing about working in sports: nearly everyone can see the results of their efforts. People want to be able to be a part of something bigger than themselves, no matter the industry.

So yes, they may do the mundane-- reimbursements, screen calls and visitors, filing, typing, airport runs, class checks... but they are also the "front line" to your program. If they have a negative attitude and frustrated vibe, they will reflect that to the recruits and parents when they're in the office visiting. Moms can get a read on them-- "Wow, they must really treat their staff poorly, their assistant looks miserable. I wonder how Coach REALLY is behind closed doors." Or, they can walk away thinking, "Wow, Coach is the real deal, everyone around the program loves being there!"

A Ted Talk titled, "What Motivates Us at Work, More Than Money" covered studies from behavioral economist Dan Ariely, found this:
- Seeing the fruits of our labor makes us more productive.
- The less appreciated we feel our work is, the more money we want to do it.
- The harder the project is, the prouder we feel.
- Knowing that our work helps others may increase our unconscious motivation.
- Positive reinforcement about our abilities increases performance.

Politics and moral of staff turns negative when only certain people are invited to team and staff social events. When possible, everyone should be invited. Some coaches consider "the team" as those on the travel roster when in reality, "the team" is EVERYONE with daily responsibilities within your program. Budgets won't always allow for it, but when possible it's worth it to make everyone on the team staff to feel as if they're part of the team! Believe me, it trickles down and can make a difference in several aspects of your program.

Start to invest those extra 5 minutes a day and chances are your assistants will go above and beyond for you those 8 hours they're at work, and they'll be a great ambassador for you and your program.

RELATIONSHIPS: YOUR COMPLIANCE OFFICE
Your Compliance Office can be an asset – not necessarily just an office trying to squash your every move. Some Compliance offices work with a different mindset than others. When you have an open relationship with your Compliance Office, they can be an asset to your recruiting efforts.

Let's face it—great recruiters are sometimes the most aggressive coaches, they toe the line. They push the farthest that they can with the rules to get even the tiniest of advantages. There's nothing wrong with this, and frankly, this is how many coaches find long-term success as a recruiter.

With your recruiting efforts, come up with some new, never-been-done ideas and ask your Compliance Office if there is a legal way to do it. It never hurts to try something new, if there is a legal way to do it.

Most NCAA rules aren't black and white, they're open to each school's interpretation, or conference's interpretation. One school may interrupt it as a no, another school may find an acceptable way to do it.

Work to have an open relationship with your Compliance staff to find a legal way to do something new—it's tough succeeding in recruiting if your Compliance Office only works from a place of "No." Find creative ways for them to say, "YES." Success in recruiting is ultimately about finding an edge. How can your Compliance Office help your efforts instead of immobilize you?

RELATIONSHIPS: UNIVERSITY STUDENT BODY
When you think about the essence of college sports, you probably envision a big, electric atmosphere with your team propelled on to a win by a big crowd, followed by a court/field storming by the boisterous student section.

This type of relationship between your team and the student body doesn't just happen, even at athletically successful and tradition-rich schools. To see these capacity crowds, you've got to put the time into recruiting your students and building this relationship. Students are finicky and have high standards: they want to be a part of a WINNING program, they want to be entertained, they want fun giveaways and they want direct interaction!

This is a relationship that requires constant effort, make time each week to interact with students. Even at schools with historic athletic success, the relationship with the student body must constantly be cultivated. Ultimately, it's not your program, it's their program! Invite students to be an integral and contributing part of your program!

KEY GROUPS:
- Band
- Cheer & Dance
- Spirit Groups & Sports Clubs
- Greeks
- Intermural Teams
- By graduating class
- All students who attend games

Thank about it – many campuses are divided. The big, popular athletes who are getting a "free education" vs. the average student. Stereotypically, it's common for tension or negativity to arise between the jocks and the Greeks, or other groups. Athletes are viewed to get preferential treatment (true or not), help break down the walls between your players and the students.

Your program (coaches and players) needs to be accessible and visible on campus – not above everyone or kept in hiding, only seen on gamedays. Take the time to be relatable and active on campus—eat where the regular students eat, show up at major campus activities and traditions – even if not specifically invited or asked. Surprise the students in the dorms or Greek courts the night before a big game, buy snacks for the super fans in the student section. Take time to thank them before or after games—encourage your team to celebrate and thank them as well. Hype them up by posting social media pics—give them shoutouts on Twitter or Instagram.

WAYS TO INTERACT WITH YOUR STUDENT FANS:
- Email invitations on key game dates (first game, rival games, conference games of major importance).
- Email thanks after big wins.
- Invite them to games via social media.
- Thank them for their support via social media, after both wins and losses
- Thank them regularly at press conferences.
- Special event for these groups in the pre-season so they can interact with team and get early look.
- Special post-season event if the team had a successful season.
- Evaluate why they do and don't attend games – do a focus group through your Marketing Department.
- Allow them special on-field access pre or post-game.
- Invite them to an open practice.
- Celebrate with them post-game.
- Involve them during games, have redshirt and injured players interact with students during the game.

RELATIONSHIPS: COMMUNITY AND FANS

With the rising cost of tickets and tight economic times, fans have a lot of options. They can watch games on TV, follow on Twitter, stream on their phones… they need a reason to purchase tickets, sit in traffic, pay to park, eat a $10 hot dog and take time out of their day to come see your team play!

Same with your student body, you'll need to actively recruit your local community to get and keep fans involved in your program. Don't just assume they'll show up, buy tickets and gear, and unconditionally support you—they won't! Even at historic programs, you'll have to put in the work!

Like recruiting prep athletes, understand that the community needs an emotional connection (and great product) to come out and support you!

Creating good will in your local community and with your fanbase also helps connect your players to the university, and enhances their college experience. Community service shows your players their leadership position in the community and helps build a sense of responsibility.

STILL MAKING GREAT TIME MANAGEMENT DECISIONS, FOCUSING MOST OF YOUR ATTENTION ON RECRUITING AND GAME PLANNING, MAKE TIME TO INTERACT WITH YOUR FANS OFTEN. CREATE WEEKLY OR GAMEDAY RITUALS TO INTERACT WITH FANS AND INVITE THEM TO BE AN ACTIVE PARTICIPANT INTO YOUR PROGRAM.

As with recruiting, you need to separate your fanbase and community into two groups – general and highly-influential fans:

- With your highly-influential boosters and fan groups, you need to devote time for important events, lunches and dinners, phone calls and meetings. Individuals or groups that can help you secure big donations or ticket sales need to feel personally connected to you and the program.
- General fans also need your time and attention but in less time-demanding ways. You won't be able to attend or support every function that you are invited to.
- Do your coordinators or assistants have the time (and personality) to take some of these semi-important appearances off your plate?
- Can you have injured players, redshirt players or walk-ons do some of your community appearances?

RELATIONSHIPS: FORMER PLAYERS
Within your program, your former players are the heart and soul of your program. And your program was (and may still be) the heart and soul of your former players' memories. To many, college was the best four years of their lives, along with the memories created with teammates. Create a 1st class former player program. You will need to reconnect with former players for internal and public support. As a program, you need to get them behind you and involved, not just financially.

RECRUITING MADE SIMPLE

There tends to be a cycle: the only communication or mail that many former players receive is for donation requests. They're not being invited to be actively involved with their time, or leadership... they're mostly being asked to write checks! In turn, players don't feel involved. To feel comfortable, they need to be personally approached and invited to be involved – and not just your former superstars! Don't assume that they still feel a connection to your program, most actually feel extremely disconnected because they have no personal interaction. They may not know any of the coaches or support staff or anyone connected to the program anymore.

Create an email newsletter that can be distributed to share timely information about the program. Let them feel like an insider, that they are getting tidbits that aren't out in the media yet, or details that aren't public yet. Invite them to "player-only" events occasionally, give them special access to practice or scrimmages.

Former players also enjoy catching up with each other and networking. Create ways for them to hear news on each other, social events for them to gather annually and professional networking opportunities.

Leave the fundraising to the Booster office, unless you are a head coach or have fundraising responsibilities. First, just work to have them feel welcome and personally invited to be a part of your program. Donors and boosters usually love hearing that former players are getting more involved personally with the program, and usually are more open to making increased donations to the program when they see alumni rallying around the team.

- **EVENTS:** Coordinate an annual event that can grow each year. Organize a picnic that can help former players to reconnect with each other, as well as reconnect with the program in the pre-season, off-season or around a rivalry game:
    - Golf Tournament
    - Happy Hour (the night before a big game or post-game)
    - Flag Football "Weekend Warrior" Tournament
    - Spring game BBQ
    - Alumni game
    - Charity Event
    - Bowling Tournament
    - Pep rally for championship reunion teams

- **JOB ASSISTANCE:** Put emphasis on helping recent graduates find professional connections within the sport or in the business world. Put time into career transitions, don't just quit your efforts for them once their eligibility is up! Follow-up with your recent grads! Keep track of former players in great "real world" positions and share these with your recruits.

• **NETWORKING:** Coordinate an Athletic Department job fair for current and recent grads. Create a LinkedIn group and invite your current and former players to join and interact. Create a directory with contact information, job titles and organizations listed so they may reach out to each other.

• **COMMUNICATION:** Send monthly or quarterly newsletters to former players with exclusive news and information that's not public knowledge yet, with upcoming important dates and team news! Make them feel like they hear occasional news first before the general public.

• **HOLIDAY GREETINGS:** Send holiday and birthday greetings via mail or email.

• **CAMPS:** Invite former great players back to work camps. Camp will be more enjoyable for campers, parents and former players have an opportunity to interact with the program behind-scenes and reconnect.

• **DATABASE:** Put together an accurate database of email addresses and mailing addresses. Reach out to the group to find lost letterwinners that you have no contact info for.

• **VIP ALUMNI:** Send handwritten notes to your VIP alumni who play professionally or are business executives. If you have pro athletes, send them hand written notes before the season begins or wish them good luck in the post-season. Send team gear.

• **SIDELINE PASSES:** Evaluate sideline pass procedures or comp ticket allowances. Work with the Athletic Director for a special invite for former players – either discounted tickets, comp tickets or sideline passes for select games or season tickets.

• **FORMER PLAYER LIASION:** Have one central person within your office, not just the Booster Office, to keep up with former player program.

RELATIONSHIPS: OTHER COLLEGE COACHES

A surprising aspect among the profession– a career that revolves around competition– is the comradery among coaches across the country. Sure, on gameday, it's everyone for themselves, but the day-to-day responsibilities can be much easier if you've built and maintained a great network of coaches across the collegiate level that you can lean on and grow with.

Attend coaching conferences, be friendly when crossing paths on the road or during gamedays, grab dinner or a beer when you see other assistants in the airport or hotel. If a team does a certain thing well, it doesn't hurt to pick up the phone or drop an email complementing their strength and ask if they had any drills they could share with you. People like to be complimented, and are often flattered to be asked for advice.

As a prospect approaches you who doesn't have the talent to play in your program but could be a good option for a friend at a lower-level school, it's a win-win to say, "Hey, I've got a buddy at _____ University who may have interest in your video-- Unfortunately, I don't think you'd be a fit for us but I'm happy to pass your information and video along." #1- It ends your time spent on a player who is not talented enough for your program. #2- It isn't a cold rejection, it may lead to a scholarship offer for them. #3- It gives you a quick reason to catch up with the other college coach. #4- It can actually help the other coach.

Other ways to strengthen those relationships: position drills, teaching materials or provide insights for job interviews. Some coaching staffs share scouting reports on mutual opponents when asked (with head coach's approval) or visit with other staffs in the offseason to learn new philosophy. Coaches may call you for good position drills or weight room guidance-- share and take a few minutes out of your day to make a connection, or make it stronger.

You don't have to always view other coaches as competitors, consider them as potential mentors, connectors or technical resources. Be friendly in interactions, responsive if they reach out to you for assistance and proactive when building a network.

> ## "MY CIRCLE IS, IN REALITY, NOT A CIRCLE. IT IS A PYRAMID."
> ## – MALCOLM GLADWELL

RELATIONSHIPS: THE PROS
Successful college coaches have great relationships with coaches across all levels-- high school, college and the pros. If you want to work at a high level, you need them all to build a great career!

If contacted by a pro scout about a current player, be direct and honest with their questions. You don't want to build a reputation of giving misinformation, causing others to make bad decisions in their own jobs. Although you may love your players, you also need to keep your credibility and not sugarcoat your player's strengths and weaknesses. Yes, they're asking for your input and thoughts on a particular player, but they're also asking several other people. You don't want to give the sugarcoated answer that doesn't fit the picture that everyone else is painting, it's better to be honest. Focus your efforts for the player to help them develop and prepare for pros before it gets to this point.

If you already have relationships with coaches, scouts or front office staff with pro teams, ask if you can get a quote for recruiting or media guide purposes about your style of play, player development, leadership or reputation.

Many pro coaches host or participate in coaching clinics or offer off-season fellowships- check their website or social media accounts. Call them, ask around!

And lastly, a lot of people are flattered when asked for advice. It never hurts to ask for teaching drills or questions about their specific philosophy or style of play. If interested, reach out via email or social media and message them about a drill or question. Keep your question simple and don't stalk, but you never know where the relationship or information can lead.

RELATIONSHIPS: RITUALS

One of the highest compliments I can give about coaches who I've worked for is that their players play hard for them and their relationships carry on past graduation. Their players respect them and they have genuine relationships. As a coach, you can't ask for more than a roster full of players who will play their hearts out for you!

Of this group of select coaches, many have consistent rituals with their players. It's human nature to look to rituals, and these are great ways to build relationships with your players.

Regularly you need to look your players eye-to-eye. You need to make "moments" together, you need to know when and how to keep your team loose. Dance, make jokes, sing, impersonations, meditations... you need to make practice and the daily grind fun.

TEAM-BUILDING RITUALS YOU CAN CREATE:
- Start & close of practice routine
- Pre-practice stretch routine
- Time in lockerroom with your players
- In your meeting room
- In-game celebrations with your position group
- End of semester grade honorees
- Quote or Thought of the Day
- First day of practice or orientation tradition
- Pre-game tradition
- Position group weekly meal
- Position group weekly off-field social outing

CHAPTER #7
SELLING PROGRAM

"It is essential to understand that battles are primarily won in the hearts of men. Men respond to leadership in a most remarkable way and once you have won his heart, he will follow you anywhere."
-VINCE LOMBARDI

"A goal without an action plan is a daydream."
-DR. NATHANIEL BRANDEN

"The more concerned we become over the things we can't control, the less we will do with the things we can control."
-JOHN WOODEN

"Opportunities don't happen, you create them."
- CHRIS GROSSER

SELLING PROGRAM: TARGET AUDIENCES

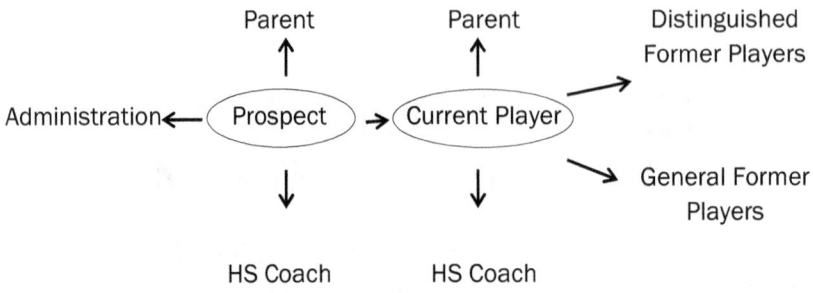

"Think on All Levels"

Example: Spring Game

HS Prospect: Send invites, market the day heavily- you want buzz with top prospects! Include time to visit with coaches, see campus, enjoy a meal and see facilities.

HS Coach: First, focus on personally inviting prep coaches of your recruits. Secondly, invite all coaches from the state and region.

HS Parent: Mail invite- market the day! Invite them to "come check us out!" Send info on "What to Expect with Recruiting," and answer commonly asked recruiting questions. Encourage them to exercise their options and do their research over the Spring and Summer!

Current Player Parents: Send invite- Plan a BBQ for player families. Don't forget about them because you've already signed their child into your program, create an event for them to gather. Develop a Parents Council, a group to coordinate away travel, fundraisers, banquets, etc.

HS Coach of Current Player: Invite them personally. They are just as proud of their players as you are, make them feel wanted so they will continue to help you sign players in the future!

Former Players: Send invite- They need to feel that they're still part of your program, and they need to hear from your office specifically. Send a letter inviting them to the game with an outlook on spring practices, with a few details not released yet to the media. If possible, plan a pre-game or post-game former player tailgate or luncheon. Coordinate coaches schedules so your staff can mingle with your former letterwinners.

EXAMPLE DAY OF SPRING GAME:
MORNING OF:
- Breakfast with recruits
- One-on-one meeting with recruits and head coach / position coaches
- Position meetings with team

LUNCH
- Team meal
- Campus tour for recruits
- HS Coaches lunch

GAME
- Recruits eat after checking in for game
- HS Coaches attend game

POST-GAME
- More one-on-one visits with recruits and head coach / position coaches
- BBQ with parents of current players
- BBQ with former players

Thinking on all three levels:

High School	University	Pros
Preseason	Pre-season	Draft
Season	Season	Pre-season
Playoffs	Post-season	Season
Championship Games	Recruiting/Signing Day	Post-season
Post-Season Awards	HS Clinics	
SAT/ACT Test Dates	Spring Practices	
Spring Practices	Graduation	
Spring Jamborees	Camps	
Graduation	Offseason workouts	
Summer Tournaments/Events	Pro Days/Draft	
Offseason workouts	Banquet	

SELLING PROGRAM: DECISION MAKERS

One of your first and most important moves in getting to know your top prospects is understanding who else will help them make their college decision. Players rarely make the decision on their own, they're getting advice, input and seeking approval from a few different key people: Mom, Dad, Coach, mentors, siblings, girlfriends/boyfriends, ministers, signs from God, etc.

Once you find out who the other key players are, recruit them too! Include these key people on visits, make time to get to know them, share your plan with them, speak of the academic opportunities, send recruiting mailouts and emails to them and occasionally handwrite personal notes to them. You may have to recruit them just as hard as you're recruiting the prospect themselves.

Don't assume that you know who the prospect will look to for advice or approval, ask them directly! "Who's going to help you make the decision? Mom? Dad? Coach?" Find out directly from the source!

SELLING PROGRAM: TOP 30 FACTORS THAT PLAYERS AND FAMILIES CONSIDER WHEN CHOOSING SCHOOLS

In alphabetical order...

- Academic Support Available for Student-Athletes
- Athletic Department Budget
- Big Name School vs. Small Name School
- Brand of Athletic Gear
- City the University is Located In
- Class Size
- Conference Strength / Level of Competition
- Consistent Success of the Athletic Department as a Whole
- Crime Rates / Safety
- Degree Programs Offered
- Distance from Home
- Draft Record
- Facilities
- Family Atmosphere
- Graduation Rates of Athletes
- Opportunity to Win a Championship
- Other Top Signees
- Personality of Head Coach
- Player Improvement / Development
- Playing Time – Opportunity to Start or Get Significant Minutes
- Post-Season Opportunities
- Program on the Rise After Tough Few Years
- Relationship with the Head Coach or Position Coach
- School Spirit
- Student Body
- Style of Play
- Team Discipline

- Traditions
- Two-Sport Athlete Opportunities
- Visibility to Help Earn National Individual Awards

SELLING PROGRAM: TIPS FOR CONVERSATIONS

DIRECT CONTACT INFO: Get their direct cell phone number and email address and confirm their correct social media accounts. Give them your direct contact info and tell them to call you whenever, especially if they are too young to contact under NCAA rules.

REMIND THEM: If it's a young, top prospect, remind them that NCAA rules prohibit when and how often you can call them. But, they can call you at any time! If very talented, encourage them to call you at a set time each week or as often they want. Remind them that you are unable to return their message, so if you happen to miss their call that they should call back.

HELP THEM REMEMBER YOU: When speaking with recruits, keep in mind that they get initially overwhelmed meeting college coaches or are hearing from several assistant coaches all at once.

As adults, how many times have you got an exciting phone call but forgot the intro as the caller announced their name? "Great news, but WHO is this," you want to ask. A lot of head coaches are national or regional names, but assistant coaches (even at major programs) are often faceless, and nameless! Help associate your name, and repeat yourself of what school you are from and what position you coach. Help them remember you by name! Tell them to save your name and school into their phone while you are on the line with them, and to call you at any time!

PUT HEAD COACH ON: Since most sports are limited by the number of times they can call prospects, get more out of your calls by putting the head coach or coordinator on the line as well. Set up time with your head coach or coordinator to make calls together.

MAKE PLANS FOR NEXT CALL: Especially when getting to know a prospect, give them a head's up about when you'll be calling again. If they're too young to contact, set up a time for them to call you next. "Good luck Friday at your tournament, give me a call Saturday and let me know how it went." Prospects are insecure and unsure, try to always set up the next call before you hang up!

WHEN ARE THEY MAKING THE DECISION: "What's your timeline, when do you plan on making the decision?" Do they want to make the decision early and wrap up the recruiting process quickly to focus on their prep season... or do they want to take their time, enjoy their high school season and decide closer to Signing Day? Flat out ask them. Remember, they're teenagers and change their mind often, but at least get some clues to when they're planning on deciding.

WHAT OTHER SCHOOLS ARE THEY CONSIDERING: Sure, for some prospects you can read about their Top 5 on the internet, or hear it from their prep coaches or parents... but always ask them directly yourself! You need to identify your key competition and it's your best bet to hear it directly from the prospect.

WHAT'S THEIR DREAM SCHOOL?: Ask them directly and they'll give you a secret roadmap. Once you know exactly what they're looking for, you can tailor your pitch to them! Distance from home, style of play, conference, academics? Find out why their dream school is their dream school and brainstorm ways to spin your opportunities to match.

WHO WILL HELP THEM MAKE THE DECISION: You know they're likely influenced by someone else, getting input and advice to make the decision. Go ahead and ask who it is, so you know who else you need to recruit. "So, who's going to be helping you make the decision? Mom? Dad? Coach?" You never know who the key player will be, who they trust and who they look to for approval. Go ahead and ask directly!

WHAT TO EXPECT DURING THE RECRUITING PROCESS: This whole process is new to a lot of prospects, ask them if they want a brief overview of what to expect. Briefly explain to them how you plan to recruit them, how scholarship offers work, timelines, upcoming events you would like them to attend, academic standards they need. Give them a quick and honest overview of the next few steps.

TURN THE TABLE: Let them ask the questions, "What questions do you have for me?" If you don't have the answer on the spot for a parent or player's question, track it down and get back to them quickly with answers. Show them that getting answers for them is a priority to you. What's important to them is important to you.

ARE YOU GETTING OUR MAIL?: If they're already on your radar and getting mail, ask them if they're receiving mail/email from you to confirm that you have the correct address. Is their prep coach passing it along, if it's being mailed to the school?

GET TO KNOW THEM: When committing, many prospects will say, "It wasn't JUST about sports with them, they cared about me as a person. We didn't just talk sports we talked life."

IN YOUR RECRUITING CONVERSATIONS, KEEP GREAT NOTES. YOU WILL BE TALKING TO HUNDREDS OF PROSPECTS THROUGHOUT THE YEAR, YOU CAN'T POSSIBLY KEEP THEM ALL STRAIGHT, ESPECIALLY BEFORE MEETING IN PERSON. MANY SCHOOLS EVEN HAVE AN INTERNAL QUESTIONNAIRE OR FOLDER THAT COACHES CAN USE TO GET TO KNOW PROSPECTS AND KEEP TRACK OF THIS INFORMATION COLLECTED THROUGH THESE CONVERSATIONS.

Don't drill them with 50 questions in one setting, but here are some examples of conversation starters you can use over time to get to know them more personally:

- Who are you closest to- a family member, a coach, a mentor?
- Who do you live with?
- What did you do last summer? Any plans for this summer?
- What are you interested in seeing on campus?
- What is your proudest achievement?
- How often do you want to hear from me?
- Are you spiritual, do you attend church?
- Tell me more about your family – Where are your parents from? Where did they go to school? Occupation? Interests? Tell me more about your siblings.
- What would you be interested in majoring in?
- What extracurricular activities are you involved in?
- Community involvement?
- Who's your favorite pro player?
- What's your favorite video game?
- What's your girlfriend/boyfriends name? How did you meet?
- What are your best weightroom lifts?
- Who is your favorite band/artist?
- Tell me about your prep coaches – where'd they go to school?
- Favorite food, snacks, drinks?
- How do you like to get info – calls, texts, mail, email, social media?
- Are there any hesitations about our program, university, coach, city?
- Have any family or friends attended the University?
- Who is your favorite coach and why?
- Do you have friends playing at other colleges? Where and what have their experiences been like?
- Who are some of the best players that you've played against?
- What's your favorite vacation spot?
- Do you have any hobbies?
- What other sports or positions did you play as a kid?
- Other than your sport, what would be your dream job?
- Do you have a PT job? What was your first job?
- What are your goals for the upcoming season/off-season and how are you preparing to meet those goals?

IN ORDER TO CONVINCE THEM THAT YOU ARE THE RIGHT CHOICE FOR THEM, YOU NEED TO UNDERSTAND THEM AND THEIR DESIRES. WHAT MAKES THEM TICK? WHAT DRIVES THEM?

WHAT'S GOING ON IN THE RECRUITS WORLD?: As we get wrapped up in our own world-- our upcoming games, our current players, our families, remember to focus conversations on what's going on in your prospects world. What's big to them right now? Prom, Homecoming, Spirit Week, SAT/ACT, rivalry games, birthdays? (See page 114.)

DETAILS: When possible, use details to show that you're really listening. It's so important to keep great notes. "Man, your guy Durant scored 40 last night! What a game!" Or, "I just saw an episode of Anthony Bourdain in Italy last night, you are going to have so much fun this summer!" People are flattered that you remember what's important to them!

> **PUT TOGETHER A COMPOSITE SCHEDULE:** Gather all of your recruit's season schedules and put them into one master Excel file so you can sort them by date and have all your recruits info at your fingertips. "Good luck tonight versus Western Tech," sounds a lot better than "Hey, umm, who do you play next?" If you have the extra help from interns or grad assistants, have them organize and update this schedule. These schedules also come in handy for planning travel days, if you have time to make a quick trip you can quickly see who is playing that day.

PROUD OF YOUR SCHOOL: You need to express and radiate how proud you are of your program, players and university. Find ways to genuinely be proud and believe in what you are selling.

WHAT YOU CAN OFFER THEM THAT SEPERATES YOU FROM THE REST: Always know your elevator pitch of the top 2-3 selling points that separate you from other schools that they are considering, and share those early to help hook the interest of a prospect.

Great recruiters don't oversell, you don't have to come out of the gates force-feeding the Top 100 things about your school in your first conversation. But, you definitely want to have your facts straight.

Relationships are often more important in the final decision than stats and facts. Players remember how you make them "feel," not necessarily what's the best decision logically or statistically.

Yes, you're technically "selling" so at some point you'll have to give your pitch... but hopefully you can give them a special pitch tailored just for them after you've learned more about how and when they'll make their decision. Take your time to get to know them.

Truthfully, outside of wins and losses, many schools offer basically the same thing. How can you separate yourself, especially from other schools you know that they're considering? Do stat research (not just with athletics, compare student body, academic and Athletic Department notes) and compare what you have to offer with what's important to them.

SELLING PROGRAM: WHAT PARENTS ARE INTERESTED IN

Parents have their own sets of concerns when evaluating programs, different from their children. Parents want to feel that you have a specific plan for their child, a vision of how their career will go from year-to-year, along with the exact steps to get them there. Parents want specifics, they want to see a plan, they want to know your vision. The more details and specifics that you can give to the families of your priority recruits, the better.

Often times, these "individualized" plans can be used for all your top players, tweaked for specific preferences here and there, but overall very similar.

Parents are focused on academics, early playing time, their child's role on the team and distance from home.

Put together a general "plan" that you can discuss during recruiting. You can make minor subtractions or additions based on each specific families concerns.

The most common visions that you will be asked to communicate for parents:

- **Location**
    - Close to home
    - Ease of travel from hometown
    - Safe city and campus
    - Ability for families to get to home and conference games

- **Academics**:
    - Prestige of Degree from University
    - National University Ranking
    - Academic Major National Ranking
    - Graduation Rates of Players Under This Coaching Staff
    - Dual-Degree Programs
    - Graduate School Opportunities
    - Selective Admissions
    - Year-to-Year Vision Academically
    - Expectations of Coaching Staff for them to be Successful
    - Tutors
    - Internship Opportunities
    - Small Class Size / Professor to Student Ratio

- **Winning**:
    - Tradition of Program
    - Championship History
    - Style of Play
    - Offense
    - Defense
    - Competitive within Conference

- **Athletics & Player Development**:
    - Great Teacher Who Will Help Child Improve
    - Leadership and Discipline Development Under a Great Mentor
    - Program Philosophy / Mission Statement
    - Has Great Resume of Past Players Coached
    - Weight Room Goals / Pics of Physical Improvements of Past Players
    - Specific Drills or Position Skills You Will Focus On and Improve
    - Past Player Improvements: Where Incoming Players Were Ranked and How They Developed Under the Head/Position Coach
    - Early Playing Time
    - Depth Chart Projecting Players' Freshman Year
    - Impact Their Child Will Personally Have on Success of Team
    - Gameday Atmosphere
    - Media Coverage
    - Individual Award Opportunities
    - Year-to-Year Vision Athletically
    - Preparing for Pros

- **Post-College Plan**:
    - **Academically**: Graduate Players, Career Placement, Job Fairs and Corporate Recruitment
    - **Athletically**: Prepared Physically for Pros, Your Relationships and Experiences with Professional Teams and Process
    - **Spiritually**: Achieved all Their Personal and Athletic Goals and Transitioned into Adulthood with Great Mentors and Leadership

SELLING PROGRAM: DAILY LIST OF TASKS

The most successful coaches are masters of time management— they don't waste more than a couple seconds on interruptions that are taking away from their time to be productive on projects that matter. As you expect your players to stick to their on-field goals, you need a similar set of daily recruiting goals that you can keep posted and visible to stay on track. Prioritize the top, most important responsibilities and post them near your desk, in your car, in your locker, even on your nightstand. Staying focused on the few things that matter will be the biggest difference-maker for your career.

DAILY RECRUITING GOALS
- Watch video of players recommended by trusted sources
- Call prospects and parents
- Make calls to prep coaches of your current recruits
- Make calls to prep coaches to find new recruits and underclassmen prospects
- Handwritten notes to select prospects, coaches and parents
- Plan recruiting travel
- Stay on top of Compliance and Business Office paperwork

DAILY COACHING GOALS
- Practice prep
- Opponent scouting
- Keep up with your current players' academics
- Keep up with your current players' off-the-field lives

FOCUS AS MUCH TIME AS POSSIBLE IN THESE AREAS:
PRACTICE/GAME PREPARATIONS, ON-FIELD COACHING AND RECRUITING.
ELIMINATE OR SHORTEN TIME SPENT ON UNNECESSARY DISRUPTIONS AND INTERRUPTS THAT DON'T FALL INTO THOSE THREE CATEGORIES.

Expect to spend at least a few hours each day on recruiting-- even during the season. You must find pockets of time to make phone calls-- before school, lunchtime, in the car, after dinner time, on the weekends. Set daily goals to make a certain number of recruiting calls each day to prospects, prep coaches and parents. Recruiting will take up a sizeable chunk of your entire day—year-round! Develop this priority list and focus on it each day!

SELLING PROGRAM: MISSION STATEMENT
Every successful organization operates under a shared set of values, goals and rules. Great teams develop these together, and these are the pillars of the program, giving EVERYONE direction and consistent decision-making standards throughout the year.

DEVELOP:
- Mission Statement as a Coaching Staff
- Annual and Quarterly Goals as a Staff
- Annual and Quarterly Goals as a Team
- Rules for the Staff
- Rules for the Team

When developing these, it's important to include all coaches, players and full time staff. When everyone is part of developing the mission statement, your team values and yearly goals, they feel more accountable. You want everyone to pull together to develop your identity, goals and standards for the season so they feel responsibility to uphold them. These aren't your rules, they are OUR rules.

These "team values" are important to your whole organization, and valuable in recruiting to communicate your most basic program identify and standards. Parents and prospects can get a quick understanding of the organization and expectations of the team and coaching staff based off these standards.

ONE OF THE FIRST AND MOST-SHARED RECRUITING PIECES WILL BE YOUR TEAM MISSION STATEMENT, GOALS AND RULES.

Annual evaluations across each position should include these guidelines, along with disciplinary issues. Clear-cut standards are easy to evaluate. They're direct, specific and more than a job description! There are specific benchmarks.

Along with sharing these expectations with recruits and their families, share throughout the facility and in coaches' offices. Keep these visible where players and staff can see them daily. Expectations are clear! Team Missions are visible in coach's offices. Team Goals are posted throughout the facility. Team Rules are posted in the lockerroom and Player Lounge. There are no surprises of what is expected.

SELLING PROGRAM: 3 WAYS YOU WANT TO BE THOUGHT OF

Your audiences will perceive you and mirror back to you what you present to them, and there are ways that you can help influence the adjectives they use to describe your program.

Winning – that's the biggest seller and it's up to you to take care of business. You can only "market" yourself for so long, you need to be able to back it up with wins ASAP!

But, as you are building a program or recruiting class, narrow down three descriptions that you would like your program to be. You may not quite be there yet, but as a staff, pick three descriptions you want people to think about your team. These need to be decided as a group.

WHAT TYPE OF PLAYERS DO YOU WANT TO ATTRACT?:
"We play / prepare harder than anyone in the country."
"We want to be the fastest team in the league."
"We are tougher than anyone in the conference."
"We have the best technique in the conference."
"We play with the most poise in the league."

Now, once you agree on your three descriptions, try to primarily use only those three descriptions when discussing your team... publicly to the media, on social media, on mailouts, in team meetings... and slowly, your audiences will begin mirroring you with their language and perception of your team. All coaches need to use the same three descriptions—you must ALL be speaking on the same few core strengths or goals.

Over and over, try to stick to only those three. Don't muddy the water with fifty different adjectives or strengths with each coach using their own. Stick to speaking up about just three!

You can help control the perception, as long as you're also putting in the work. Obviously, you can't say you're the toughest team in America if your players are soft. Pick three truths, or near-truths, "We are working to be the _____ team."

You can slowly help define the way your team is perceived among recruits and your fans, as long as you can eventually back it up on the field.

SELLING PROGRAM: CONTROL THE MESSAGE
The good thing about today's instant world of social media is that these platforms help you to control the message about your program directly. While the media is out there writing about your program in their own way (or just not writing about you at all), you need a very thoughtful plan to help market your program to the type of players you want to recruit.

It's a good idea to have a point person who is the organizer of recruiting marketing. They can pick out pictures, request more pictures, order displays for the offices and facility, come up with selling points. Promote these messages via mailouts, social media and email blasts. They coordinate the marketing aspect of recruiting.

You need to develop and convey precise messages and have great pictures. Every decision about your program from the lockerroom design to the mailouts to the office pictures need to be made with recruiting in mind. Among great recruiting staffs, nearly every non-coaching decision is based on recruiting. EVERY decision based on what is best for recruiting. Today is already here, what decisions can help us with the next few signing classes?

Promote, promote, promote these aspects of your program!

SELLING PROGRAM: ACADEMICS
Along with pictures of key athletic moments around the facility, parents and recruits need to see your pride and success with the ultimate reward – a college degree! You need to be just as proud of their academics as you are of their athletics.

In your office, display pictures of you with your graduates and their families on graduation day. Around the facility, have a dedicated display with a list of your staff's graduates (from that university) and their major. Make sure to get great group pictures of your graduates each year and rotate them in prominent displays within the facility.

These displays will become a sense of pride and motivation for your current players, and convey to your recruits and their parents that you are serious about their academic and personal success.

SELLING PROGRAM: PROMOTE THE HEAD COACH
When marketing your program emphasize your head coach, their philosophy and plan, and the value and importance of their interaction with prospects.

It's an honor for the head coach to get involved in recruiting and promote this to your recruits. Promote your head coach's excitement and interest in meeting them and getting to know them better.

Even if you personally are focused on becoming a head coach eventually, remember that it's your head coaches' program, and always promote their accomplishments first and foremost.

SHARE SUCCESS OF YOUR HEAD COACH:
- Improvements the program has made under the head coach
- Head coach's career accomplishments
- Antidotes about the head coach personally
- Relationship head coach has with their players
- Relationship head coach has with their former players
- Relationship head coach has with pros
- Success head coach has had developing players over their career
- Role head coach plays off-the-field in their players' lives
- Head coach as a family person—their spouse and kids are active in the program
- Head coach as a college player

SELLING PROGRAM: DEVELOPING MARKETING YOUR SELLING POINTS

SELLING POINTS:
Competition is intense between programs across ALL levels. Even at elite programs, universities that seem like they would be an easy sell: they're in heated competitions with 3-5 other elite schools for their top prospects. Believe me, no coach or school has it "easy!" For this reason, you need to find every edge possible to separate yourself!

When building relationships with prospects and their families your first overall goal is to get them to campus. If you can get them to campus, you have a shot! To lure them to campus you need to show them what you have to offer through great pictures and key selling points. Top selling points need to cover academics, player development, path to a championship, playing time, conference affiliation and of course, win percentage and recent championships!

The best recruiting coaches are marketing geniuses. Just as much as they are X's & O's masters, they knew exactly what they have to offer and exactly how to pitch it to their different audiences. And they are pitching at all times: graduation speeches, booster club speeches, press conferences, media interviews. Nearly every time great recruiters open their mouths away from the facility, they speak as if they are speaking directly to a huddle full of prospects. You never know who is listening!

> **AS A STAFF, YOU NEED TO ANNUALLY SIT DOWN AND DEVELOP YOUR PROGRAM'S "SELLING POINTS," THAT CAN HELP DRAW THEM TO CAMPUS FOR A VISIT. SELLING POINTS ARE YOUR TOP MARKETING POINTS, THE KEY THOUGHTS YOU WANT TO STICK IN THE MINDS OF PROSPECTS AND THEIR FAMILIES.**

Salespeople have their elevator pitch memorized-- one sentence detailing why you should choose their product. You definitely need to develop and memorize your elevator pitches as well too! You will need to develop a few different top pitches based on the needs of the different types of prospects that you are recruiting.

Take each key decision factor and find hard analytics, exact numbers to share (as long as these numbers are impressive). Compare your research to other schools or more specifically, compare them to the handful of schools that your top prospects are considering.

There are several ways to "spin" your selling points– nationally, in conference, in-state, among public/private schools. Take a deeper look to see how you can tweak your selling point to make them sound even more impressive!

EXAMPLE:
- We are #2 in the conference in Graduation Rates
- We are #5 in FBS in attendance
- We are #2 in the nation in number of majors offered
- We are #12 among public schools nationally in freshman retention rates
- We are #1 in the state in win % over the last 10 years
- We are #1 among schools you are considering in student to faculty ratio

You need to put together a simple Top 10 list of your best recruiting selling points, for parents and for prospects. Ask your Sports Information Director to help you brainstorm or research stats. Give them some direction as to what areas are important to your recruits.

180 WAYS TO MARKET YOUR PROGRAM

SOME FACTORS APPLY, SOME MAY NOT... WHAT TO TWEET, INSTAGRAM, MAIL OUT, EMAIL TO PROSPECTS AND THEIR PARENTS

ARE YOU A NATIONAL LEADER, LEADER WITHIN THE CONFERENCE?:

- Academic advising bullet points – technology, space, tutors available
- Academic Honor Roll
- Academic Progress Rate – National or conference rank
- All-conference players in school history or under head/assistant coach
- All-tournament team players
- Alumni in the corporate world
- Apparel contract of team
- Attendance records
- Average salary of new grad
- Banquet pictures
- Big city or college town backdrop
- Body composition analysis and improvements
- Bowl trips or in-season tournaments / locations
- Campus diversity
- Campus pictures
- Campus traditions
- Career development opportunities within major
- Career wins- head coach
- Celebrities / Former players who attend games or have visited program
- CEOs / Corporate leadership who are alumni
- Cheer / dance / mascot pictures
- Coaches interviews with national media
- Coaching pedigree of head coach – who have they learned under?
- Coaching tree of head coaches – assistants they have produced and where they are now?
- Community Service of Players and Team
- Compare program before and after head coach arrived (wins, beating ranked teams, conference success, all-conference players)
- Conference Strengths
- Cost of degree from the university – tuition, room and board, etc.
- Cost per student invested academically (budget divided by student-athletes)
- Defensive philosophy
- Degrees
- Dining Halls
- Diversity of campus
- Dorms
- Draft picks from conference – total and high rounds

- Dual-sport athletes – current and former
- Ease of travel to big cities or recruiting hotbeds
- Facilities
- Former players donating back to program
- Former players in All-Star games
- Former players in playoffs
- Former players who have won national awards or were finalists
- Fortune 500 companies who recruit university job fairs
- Gameday traditions
- Graduation pictures of athletes
- Graduation pictures of notable alumni walking across stage
- Graduation rates of head coach
- Graduation Success Rate – National or conference rank
- Head coach pictured with celebrities or athletes
- Head coach's wins – over ranked teams or rank compared to conference or national competitors
- Home attendance numbers – compare nationally or within conference
- In-conference opponents
- Internship opportunities through university or town
- Job fairs at university – companies who recruit there
- Legendary alumni from school – Business leaders, celebrities, etc.
- Legendary athletes from school
- List of majors – highlight most interesting
- Local top professional players
- Media coverage — behind-the-scenes pictures of photo shoots or interviews
- Motivational quotes
- National awards – nominees, finalists, winners
- National powerhouse or presence
- National ranking of specific majors within university
- National or conference record-holders
- National titles of conference or team
- National university ranking – where ranks nationally or in conference
- Newspaper articles about program – National media spotlight or great articles
- Nutritional counseling
- Offensive philosophy
- Offseason training
- Online tour of campus
- Pep rallies
- Pictures of coaches and family
- Pictures of coaches with fans and students interacting
- Pictures of magazine covers / website coverages
- Pictures of players with fans and other students celebrating
- Pictures of town

- Position-by-position: Great former players at each position
- Plan for development
- Player development plan or history of staff
- Player stats – conference or national leaders or ranking
- Players named all-conference Player of Week or Player of Year
- Players on student-athlete advisory committees
- Players to professional contracts opportunities
- Playing time and stats graduating – opportunity open by position
- Position-by-position former player leaders or legends
- Post-playing career / job placements
- Post-Season appearances
- Practice facility
- Preseason rankings
- Pro Day pictures
- Pro draft streaks
- Pro players actively competing
- Pro players in post-season
- Pro players voted All-Star or All-Conference
- Pro players—full list of past and present
- Pro players or alumni who train on campus in off-season
- Pro scouts who've attended games recently
- Profiles or Q&As with assistant coaches or coordinators
- Putting together a top recruiting class – be a part of it and make history
- Quotes from articles from media members, opponent coaches, current players, opponent players
- Quotes from current players about head coach, team or teammates
- Quotes from former players in pros about program, head coach or current players
- Quotes from TV announcers
- Ranking – National or conference
- Ranking streaks from recent years
- Ranking of fanbase merchandise sales
- Recent win streaks
- Records set under head coach
- Rival game pictures
- Roster / Depth chart
- Season outlook
- Senior class
- Schedule
- Small class sizes
- Social media accounts – number of followers if high
- Social media accounts of each coach of your sport
- Social media accounts of university, athletic department and team
- Speakers or leaders who have visited university

- Stadium or arena expansions
- Stadium or arena luxury suites and alumni rooms
- Stadium or arena pictures
- Staff continuity – how long have assistants and head coaches worked together combined
- Strength of schedule
- Student / fan section pictures
- Student athletes elected to campus leadership
- Student-Faculty ratio
- Success of other teams in Athletic Department
- Team GPA – Improvement or record?
- Team or athletic department Hall of Fame inductees
- Team values or mission statement
- Teammates
- Team websites
- Traditions
- Town highlights or landmarks
- Training table and individualized nutritional planning
- TV contract money
- TV network associated with conference
- TV games – total numbers or percentages
- Tweets from celebrities or former players about program
- Uniform designs
- University selection rates (if high)
- Upcoming games: Dates, opponent, TV/Radio, time
- Upcoming schedules
- Weather
- Weightroom improvements including pictures of before and after
- Weight room measurements
- Weightroom philosophy
- Weightroom pictures
- Willingness to play freshmen by coaching staff
- Win streaks of head coach
- Winning percentage – head coach
- Wins – point margin of wins
- Wins over ranked teams

ADDITIONAL IDEAS FOR MAIL OR EMAILS...

- 100 days until... Practice Starts, First Game, Graduation, Signing Day, Etc.
- ACT/SAT date and signup reminders
- Alma Mater
- Camp brochure
- Camp dates

- Campus move-in day
- Congrats on High School Playoffs
- Congrats on Pre-Season Rankings
- Elite camp invite
- Goal setting
- Good luck on high school season
- Happy Birthday
- Happy Holidays – Holidays, Thanksgiving, Valentine's Day, Halloween
- Junior Day Invite
- Leadership Tips
- NCAA Eligibility Requirements
- NCAA Rules
- Personal profiles of current players, coaches and former players
- Recruiting Calendars/Definitions
- Sample Class Schedule
- Sample Daily Schedule
- Spring game / Midnight Madness Attendance Numbers
- Team picture
- Team poster
- Upcoming games – mail, email, social media
- What to expect during recruiting process

YOU NEED TO THINK ON THE SEVERAL LEVELS. YOUR MAILOUTS SHOULD REFLECT WHAT IS GOING ON AT YOUR SCHOOL, AT THE HIGH SCHOOL LEVEL AND PRO LEVEL, AND HOW THAT TIES IN TO YOUR PROGRAM.

QUOTES:
Gather positive quotes about your head coach, assistant coaches, players, University and Athletic Department throughout the year and keep a running file. These quotes can be pulled from newspaper articles, media sources, Twitter, TV/Radio broadcasts, opponent coaches.

PICTURE LIBRARY: Along with developing top selling points, you need to gather great pictures-- campus shots, gameday pageantry shots, player celebrations, coaches in action, graduations, championships. Your SID should have a photo library, along with the university communications office or the internet.

Once you get your list of top selling points together, sit down with your SID and put together a "Wish List" of photos that you need more of. Most Sports Information Departments employ professional photographers to shoot the needs of the department—schedule a meeting to see if they can help you get started. Give them a specific list of shots you would like... and be as specific as you can! Have an assistant coach or support staff supervise this library and work with the SID office to get exactly what you need. If you have the recruiting budget, hire someone for a day or afternoon to get the campus and updated facility shots that you need.

GRAPHIC DESIGN: Once you get your list of selling points together and some "WOW" photos, find someone who can help you put everything together with cool designs– a graphic design staffer, an SID who has time, a graphic design student intern.

Simple designs can still make an impact, you don't necessarily have to spend a ton of money to have impressive marketing pieces! Use big "WOW" pictures, a few catchy fonts and your logo! Keep it simple!

Come up with preferred fonts, colors, logos and design preferences or templates to produce a consistent style for your marketing pieces.

GREAT SELLING POINTS
+ WOW PICTURES
+ GRAPHIC DESIGN
= GOAL TO GET THEM TO CAMPUS

DISTRIBUTING SELLING POINTS: Once you start to get these selling points and pictures gathered and someone to help you with putting together nice graphics, plan to use them for mailouts, emails, social media, office decorations and more.

To justify these efforts and expenses, you can also use everything for multiple purposes– for your team's social media accounts for fans, for website content. Use some of these "selling points" publically to help spread the word in your region about your program, generating more interest and excitement for your program in the region.

WAYS TO DISTRIBUTE KEY SELLING POINTS:
- Team social media accounts
- Through coaches' social media accounts
- Feature stories on website or game program
- Feature videos for website / social media
- SID game notes
- Digital boards at home games (speak with Marketing Department to see if they have space to include)
- Ad space within athletic facility (speak with Marketing Department to see if they have space to include)
- Billboards in key recruiting areas
- Academic logo to be used online, in game notes, on business cards and in email signatures
- In player bios

Your SID and University Communications Office can help push these points in their game notes, through social media and press releases to get picked up by the media and fans. Enlist their help to get your recruiting messages out there!

<u>HOW OFTEN</u>:
Depending on your staffing, you need to send communication pieces weekly or daily to your top prospects. Put together a quarterly or monthly snapshot for your head coach of exactly how many prospects fall into each rating code, and an average of how many communication pieces they are receiving each week.

- **Handwritten notes**
- **Form Letters and Flyers**
- **Emails**
- **Social Media**
- **Calls & Texts** (if allowed)

TYPES OF COMMUNICATION PIECES THAT RECRUITS SHOULD RECEIVE
(MAIL, EMAIL, SOCIAL MEDIA) **:**
    1) **Motivational:** Motivate your recruits through the season, pre-season, off-season with great quotes or sayings!
    2) **Selling Points:** Upcoming games (date, opponent, location, TV) that go out with game invites. Also, keep kids in the know with what's new on campus or within your program!
    3) **Events:** Invites for Games, Practice, Camp, Junior Days, etc.
    4) **Congrats:** Acknowledge their Player of the Week honors, All-State recognition, All-County recognition, All-Star Game Invites. Recognize their achievements!

IF YOU KEEP YOUR EYES AND EARS OPEN, YOU WILL BEGIN TO REALIZE THAT THERE IS GOOD NEWS EVERY DAY WITHIN YOUR ORGANIZATION— FIND OUT WHAT IS NEW AND EXCITING AT YOUR PROGRAM, YOUR ATHLETIC DEPARTMENT, YOUR UNIVERSITY AND YOUR CITY!

SELLING PROGRAM: MASTER FILE OF SELLING POINTS
As your staff is gathering selling points, it's a good idea to have a centralized file or person keep track of all of them for future use! Be efficient and get the most out of your best selling points! Update them year-to-year to make sure they are current!

Once you begin looking and thinking on this level, you will find great information and stats that can help everyone recruit. Pool together your information as a staff!

SELLING PROGRAM: ALL-DEPARTMENT MARKETING MEETING
Looking to refresh your recruiting pitches? Order some pizzas and invite a focus group to help you. Invite key people from your program and University that you work with throughout the year: trainers, professors, academic counselors, nutritionists, secretaries, admissions counselors, Deans, equipment staff, Office of Student Life staff, Alumni Office staff, Athletic Booster Office staff. If you feel comfortable, hold a separate session with current players or parents or invite a few to the focus group.

You are in your routine. You know your circle of contacts, you are repeating the same points over and over, year-to-year. Bring in some new perspectives! Campuses are always changing, find out what is new, fresh and ground-breaking that separates you from every other program!

YOU CAN NEVER HAVE TOO MANY SELLING POINTS AS YOU TAILORING RECRUITING PITCHES TO A VARIETY OF INDIVIDUAL PLAYERS!

Some of the best ideas can come from the people that you least expect. Others may provide insight into how others perceive your program or may know of new campus initiatives, projects, technologies, alumni highlights, equipment additions or other selling points that could be valuable to your efforts!

SELLING PROGRAM: PAGENTRY OF PROGRAM
The "college experience" is an excellent recruiting tool, the pageantry that surrounds college athletics is what it's all about, and something that we lose sight of when we are loaded down with responsibilities, stress and 18-hour work days, especially after a 10+ year career!

Build it and they will come! Chances are, your traditions for players, fans, former players and alumni may have become a little stagnant. You can easily inject some excitement, energy and publicity into your program by creating new events to generate buzz about your program! It's human nature to look forward to rituals – create some new ones!

Update these areas by working with your Athletic Marketing Department to implement new interactive experiences:

ACADEMICS
- Freshmen Orientation
- Graduation Festivities

GAMEDAY PAGENTRY
- Pregame Activity with Team
- Postgame Activity with Team
- Rivalry Games
- Night before Games
- Homecoming
- Senior Day
- Parents Weekend
- Spring Game

STUDENT BODY RELATIONSHIPS
- Gameday experience
- Pre-game experience
- Post-game experience
- Closed Practice invitation
- Thank you event with band, cheerleaders, spirit groups
- Head coach's involvement at annual campus activity
- Annual event for athletes of all sports

FORMER PLAYERS
- Legendary former players who come to motivate the team
- Tailgate
- Networking opportunities
- Special events
- Closed practice invitation
- Networking opportunity for them as group
- Pre-game recognition on-field
- Homecoming event
- Thank you on scoreboard & announcement at game
- Quarterly Newsletter
- Letter from Head Coach on state of the program
- Letter from Head Coach inviting them to games

UNIVERSITY ALUMNI
- Top business alumni invited to come speak to the team
- Closed practice invitation
- Letter from the head coach on state of the program
- Letter from the head coach inviting them to games

SIGNING DAY
- Gathering / Pep Rally for fans

BUDGET RESTRAINTS LEAD TO BRAINSTORMING AND CREATIVITY. WHAT CAN YOU DO FOR LESS, BUT STILL HAVE AN IMPACT? DRAW OUT THE CREATIVITY OF YOUR STAFF!

SELLING PROGRAM: TIME TO BUILD
Never promise a prospect or their family something that you can't deliver on, it's a rookie mistake to make. To build trust, be honest. When taking over a program, it's okay to be honest that things aren't where you want them to be now, but that your staff is working hard to get everything turned around and your track record of success doing so in the past!

Instead of lying or making empty promises, market your PLAN when taking over a job, your development plan for the program. Changes will not happen overnight, it's much more believable if you can showcase your methodical (and even better, PROVEN) plan to help transition them from a great prep player to an impactful college player, and the transition steps that the program will go through during the next six months, next season and next year.

SELLING PROGRAM: OFFICIAL VISITS
Outside of gamedays, Official Visits are your most important events of the year! In some cases, you will work over a year to get a prospect to take an in-depth visit, and once they are there, you only have 48 hours to make your impression! With every detail pre-planned and double-checked, Official Visits should be stress-free, enjoyable and informative for the prospects and their families. No detail can be left to chance and you don't have a minute to waste!

TYPES OF VISITS:
- **IN-SEASON VISITS**: It's a tremendous recruiting tool to have prospects visit during a home game, particularly a big rivalry game. You are also taking a chance that they may be in the stands during a home loss, surrounded by angry fans, but it's usually a good chance to take! The excitement of gameday is a great atmosphere for prospects to experience, but you may need to compensate for the lack of personal and face time that you get to spend with your prospects while busy with team meetings, the game and gameday responsibilities. Schedule only your top recruits on Official Visits during the season, and plan ways to get ahead with your gameday responsibilities so that you can spend relaxing quality time with the prospects while they are on campus.

- **CLOSE TO SIGNING DAY VISITS**: These prospects are bouncing from one school to another during the last weeks before Signing Day, you must separate yourself as an overall elite or up-and-coming program. Your staff needs to be able to provide personal attention and you must be ready to show off your program and university. If the season is over, you must re-create the gameday environment!

DETAILS TO PREPARE PRIOR TO YOUR PROSPECT ARRIVING TO CAMPUS:

- **BACKGROUND INFO**: Gather all info needed for visit paperwork (SS #'s, addresses, legal names, etc.). Check with your Compliance Office and Business Office of all required information from prospects.

- **PAPERWORK**: Follow up with the Compliance Office and Academic Advisors for each individual. Also send all correspondence to the recruit including Five Visit Letter, daily itineraries, flight information, directions to meeting location.

- **COSTS**: NCAA rules limit what costs can be covered for who. To be sure that everyone is clear, make prospects or their families aware of costs that may need to be paid by additional guests, or for additional activities not covered on Official Visits. You don't want them to be surprised or caught off guard once they're already on campus.

- **SELLING POINTS**: Focus on the two or three areas that are really important to your prospect and their family. Make sure they walk away from your program with all of their questions answered. Spend quality time on what is most important to them, and whatever time is left on what you think are the most impressive areas of your program. Showcase all the great things you have to offer and emphasize that you are just waiting for a great player like them to help lead you to the next level of success. Invite them to become an integral part of your program.

- **ITENERARY IDEAS**:
    - Be sure to include the names of each prospect and their guests, along with relationship to the prospect. Include host names and their phone numbers, along with cell phone numbers of key staff members and coaches.

    - If hosting several prospects, put together a composite schedule so staffers can see when and where everyone should be at any time during the visit.

    - Be sure all coaches and staffers back at the office have a copy of the itinerary, along with all player hosts. If necessary, have a support staff member check in with player hosts to be sure they're on time.

- Possible stops on the itinerary:
    - Your field or arena
    - Your lockerroom, training room, weight room and team meeting rooms
    - A meal in the nice booster room with the player's favorite food catered
    - Another athletic event on campus
    - Equipment and gear
    - Skybox or luxury suites tours
    - Dorm tour
    - Athletic training room tour
    - Academic facilities tour
    - General campus tour: Student Union, Dining Halls, Intermural Facilities, Campus Gym, Bookstore
    - Plenty of snacks and mini-meals, all their favorite foods or popular foods of your city or region
    - Practice
    - Time with players

- **OVERALL PICTURE**: Emphasize that your administration and fans are willing to do what it takes to make your program top-notch, everything that your players need is at their fingertips! You have a tremendous network of alumni and boosters behind you. Your graduates earn respected diplomas.

- **PERSONAL CONNECTIONS**: Champions need champion teammates. Elite players from across the country, region or state will dedicate their four years to winning a championship. You will be surrounded by motivated teammates, who share team goals, when celebrating a conference and national title. Your talents will be developed by some of the best coaches in the country. Away from home, these coaches will have your best interests in mind throughout your career here.

- **SMALLEST OF DETAILS PLANNED OUT**: Every detail needs to be evaluated prior to their arrival. You want their arrival to be smooth, their drive to take them through a "college town," their hotel stay to be impressive, clean and comfortable. You want to make them feel relaxed and among family. When all is said and done, they can leave in a few years with a prestigious degree, a championship and success at the next level- in the job market or the professional sports.
    - Pre-Visit Information (Five Visit letter, travel information, itineraries, etc)
    - Hotel Arrangements
    - Cash Advances
    - Host Assignments
    - Meals and Snacks
    - Stadium/Facilities Presentations
    - Buses/Motorpool Vehicles- How will you get around campus and city?
    - Appointments with Athletic Department Staff and University Officials
    - Ticket Requests
    - Master Keys and Contact info for Emergencies
    - Music in Stadium/Arena
    - Phone Numbers of Key People: Coaches, Recruits, Player Hosts, Appointments, Athletic Department Staff

- **Follow-up**: Send a follow-up Thank You card signed by everyone to prospect and their family members. Continue to emphasize the plan that you have for them!

SELLING PROGRAM: UNOFFICIAL VISITS

Before the formality of an Official Visit, getting a prospect to campus for a game or other event can greatly increase your chances of getting on their list of top schools that they're legitimately considering. You want to build a buzz about your program with the top recruits within the state and region, and even nationally. You want to start building that relationship with your program early, creating an "open door" invite for your top prospects as early as possible.

THOUGHTS TO CONSIDER FOR UNOFFICIAL VISITS:
- Prepare Invite Lists & Confirmation Lists for HS Prospects and Coaches
- Game-by-Game Confirmations
- Ticket Request Confirmations & Procedures for Ticket Office
- Sideline Passes and Post-Game Procedures: Who Will Escort Which Prospects Where and When to Get to Coaches Before and After Games?
- Directions & Parking Info
- Liaison for Head Coach to Get Top Recruits in Attendance to One-on-One Meetings. Introduce coach's family to recruits family. Schedule Recruit Individual Meetings with the Head Coach, Coordinator and Position Coach.
- Who Will Hire, Train and Supervise Student Workers and Interns?
- Meal Coordinator: Who will be in Charge of Catering Orders, Set Up, Payment by Recruits, Clean-Up and Paperwork Tracking?
- Who Will Be Available to Troubleshoot?
- Rivalry games: Have a Ticket Request Plan as There Will Be a Limited Number of Tickets Available. Be Aware of Prep Coaches and Non-Priority Recruits Who Only Want to Visit During Rivalry Games and Have a Policy Set Up.

- **GAMEDAYS**: A list of priority sophomores, juniors and seniors (and even some freshmen) needs to be developed, and begin inviting those players to campus for a gameday. As a staff, decide if you will invite several players for Unofficial Visits on gamedays (better if you are a new staff taking over a program) or if you make the invite list more exclusive (for staffs who are more familiar with their region). You want your priority prospects to make it to as many games as possible, without interfering with their current season.

You need an organized check-in system if hosting several players for gamedays, with every detail worked out ahead of time. Does the Ticket Office have a limited number of recruit and high school coach tickets allotted, how selective do you need to be? Are their particular games that you will have a very limited number of recruit tickets available?

While they're on campus, you want to be able to squeeze in as much as possible! For your top prospects, this may be your only chance to get them to campus if they are being recruited by several schools. First and foremost, let them soak in the gameday atmosphere. Beyond that, ask them if there is anyone or anything in particular that they want to see or meet while on campus.

- **PRACTICE**: Invite your local prospects to practice, along with area and statewide prep coaches. Create an "open door" policy, or invite them to specific dates that the head coach prefers. Be sure prospects and coaches have good directions, a contact phone number, parking instructions and time they need to arrive.

- **JUNIOR/SOPHOMORE DAYS**: Organize an event that draws in a group of top or potential prospects for a busy weekend on campus during the off-season. Keep a list of upcoming Unofficial Visit weekends – aim to plan around one per month during the off-season to be flexible with player and prep coach schedules.

- **INDIVIDUAL UNSOLICTED CAMPUS VISITS**: Numerous HS players will want to check out the program in the summer and throughout the year. These players will be shown facilities, given a campus map and University information. Have a grad assistant or support staff give a quick, generic tour of facilities. Most likely they will bring video- either way, get them a questionnaire, encourage them to send video, play hard, have a great season, get their grades and keep in touch.

BE SURE TO BE AWARE OF DEAD PERIODS, DATES WHEN PROSPECTS MAY NOT MEET WITH COACHES ON (OR OFF) CAMPUS.

- **CAMPS**: For many programs, camps are essential. You need to aim to get your best kids into camp! Get info out to the top kids in the state, region or country and once there, create a fun, memorable experience for them.

    TIPS TO FOR CAMP SUCCESS:
    - Put together a comprehensive FAQ sheet for parents to help cut down on calls and emails to the office, be sure your camp brochure and website are detailed! Give them as much information as possible, even overgive. Dates, check-in times, prices, deposit information, online registration website, contact email for questions, camp phone number, registration deadlines, overnight accommodations for campers, local hotels for parents, roommate preferences, what the cost includes, ages/grades that sessions are open to, instructors, meal descriptions, travel info (bus, airport, train stations), what to pack, check-in times, directions, where to park, cancelation/refund policy, how campers are divided by age, sample daily schedule, costs of meals if parents eating, etc.

    - Gather all necessary information needed for registration, insurance, compliance and business office needs. Liability waiver approved by Athletic Department, medical physicals, parent signature, insurance info, camper date of birth, grade, shirt/short size, parent name, emergency contact, credit card information, etc.

    - Make parents aware of Award Ceremony times and locations, actively invite them to attend!

- Have detailed directions available online and on the brochure from points North, South, East and West. Directions from the airport, bus station, train station.

- For Team Camps, work ahead of time with each prep coach to gather all vital information. It's a headache if coaches show up the day of the camp with 30 registration forms and payments to process. Checks will bounce, credit cards will be declined, etc. It's vital that check-in is smooth and give time to your administrative staff to enter all the critical information into a database or to get the applications into alphabetical order. It's better to be organized at check-in to avoid issues than to be laid-back and let coaches just walk up with registrations. Schedule times for when each team will be arriving, stager if possible to allow time for each team to register.

- Speak with your Compliance Office about pro-rating camp sessions, if the head coach wants to offer that option. Put together a form that will be easy to process payments: Check off a session attended, with costs for meals, t-shirts, etc listed on the form to avoid financial or Compliance issues. Communicate all of the costs to your priority recruits and their families so there will be no surprises at check-in, be clear on who needs to pay for what.

- Assign all coaches, grad assistants, staffers and visiting coaches responsibilities and meet ahead of time to outline assignments. Who will stay in the dorms, handle wake-up calls, trainer schedules, transportation, walking groups from practice to dining halls/dorms, coordinate snacks, roll call, speakers, dismissal procedures, award ceremony, clinic for prep coaches, social time for prep coaches, automobile check-in of prospect cars, valuables check-in, camp bank, camp store, camp rules, camp do's and don'ts, team assignments for registered campers with coach assignments, staff meals, etc.

- Be clear with all coaches as to what is allowed and what is not allowed recruiting-wise while prospects are on campus.

- Put together a list of know prospects who will be in attendance at camp and distribute to coaching staff.

- Cross-check contact information gathered at camp with your recruit database. Fill in addresses, phone numbers, email addresses and coach info with data gathered from registration!

SELLING PROGRAM: CAMPUS TOURS

The truest test for recruits is their comfort level once they're on campus. A school may catch their interest from afar-- through social media, websites and guidebooks but not "feel right" in person. The people, the vibe, the attitude and spirit make a place! Sure, you want to win them over logically but you must also win their hearts! Shape visits on the "feel" of your campus and program. They have to want to be there to choose you over all the other schools. They need to love the vibe, feel the spirit and attitude of the lockerroom, campus and town! They need to "Fit in."

• <u>ITENERARY</u>: Parents love details and recruits want to know what to expect. A day or two before their visit, send a detailed itinerary including what hotel they way will be staying at (if applicable), where you will meet them, cell phone numbers of staff members, and a list of stops they will be making throughout the visit – attending a game, campus tour, dorm visit, faculty meeting, head coach meeting, meals, free time.

• **DRIVE FROM AIRPORT TO CAMPUS**: When transporting recruits from the airport to campus or when driving from location to location throughout the weekend-- keep your routes away from bad parts of town, even if it means making a longer trip. Make sure that everyone is seeing a safe, clean, vibrant community, even if the campus borders on some tough neighborhoods. Do a test drive ahead of time, find the best routes visually for your weekend itinerary to and from all points of interest.

• **IF YOU STAY READY, YOU DON'T NEED TO GET READY**: I can't tell you the number of times that a prospect has called—they just happen to be in town and want to stop by before heading back home. Are your offices and facilities visit-ready at a moment's notice? Make it a habit of keeping all spaces clean and ready for visitors.

• **NO DETAIL LEFT TO CHANCE**: Once details are lined up—prepare and share itineraries with prospects, staff, family. Confirm appointments and have cell phones of all appointments on itineraries so there is no confusion or wasted time. Have an intern or assistant one step ahead of the group on the itinerary to take care of any issues ahead of time.

• **FOCUS ON THE PEOPLE, NOT NECESSARILY THE PLACES**: To win their hearts you need to further cement the emotional connection they have with your program. Interactions need to be personalized, intimate and direct. They need one-on-one attention from key people, depending on their decision factors:

- Player Hosts - Similar Personalities, Hometowns, Positions.
- Head Coach
- Position Coach
- Other Assistant Coaches
- Athletic Director
- Strength & Conditioning Staff
- Professors and Deans from their Preferred Major
- Nutritionists
- Training Staff
- Academic Staff
- Sports Information Staff
- College Fanbase
- Student Groups

- **SPOTLESS & SHINY**: Offices, lockerrooms, meeting rooms, weight rooms, kitchens, training rooms, bathrooms and dorms need to be spotless for visits! The day or two before Official and Unofficial Visit weekends, be sure to alert building housekeeping to take extra care. If possible, have carpets shampooed, floors freshly waxed, fields painted, lights replaced and chips in the paint fixed.

Year-round, have current players keep the lockerrom tidy and have lockers spotless. You should have a regular team policy of how lockers should look- a tidy, minimalist setup. You may not have notice when prime visitors are coming!

The day of Official or Unofficial Visits, do a sweep to make sure that every stop is spotless: the garbage is taken out, there are no dirty dishes in the sink, empty shipping boxes are broken down and at the dumpster, there is no debris on the carpet, desks are tidy, carpets are clean and bathrooms are spotless. Even after housekeeping has cleaned, take another look around - you never know what has taken place after-hours. The morning of, do a building walk-through.

If necessary, send an email to staff alerting them of your incoming special guests and ask that all areas remain clean and projects postponed on that date.

- **ACADEMICS**: Set up meetings with professors or deans within their desired major. Gather up your top academic selling points relating to program rankings, academic support, internship opportunities, career placement assistance, corporate recruiting, networking opportunities and more.

- **HIGHLIGHT STRENGTHS, HIDE WEAKNESSES**: If certain areas of your program are behind the times and in major need of renovation, keep tours brief or completely away from those areas unless recruits specifically request to go there. Bring them to the shiny parts of your program instead, they likely won't notice what you aren't showing them. Accentuate the positive and bypass the outdated!

- **THOROUGH BUT NOT BORING**: It's important that the prospects and their families feel like they're seeing all of your great facilities and traditional campus spots without boring them with too many stops. As a staff, develop a list of must-see facility and campus stops, practice tours as a staff and with other grad assistants and interns who may give tours. Create in-depth tours for your priority recruits and shorter basic tours for less priority recruits. Focus on creating a sense of "this is what college sports is all about" and emphasizing an exciting campus life.

- **FOCUS ON GROWTH AND IMPROVEMENTS**: Recruits and parents like to feel like they're arriving on campus at the right time-- there's a buzz, there's new construction. Money is flowing in and building fresh, upgraded spaces! Walk them through the dust and tell them how many millions are being spent! If a new campus building or athletic facility has been discussed or is in the early planning stages, follow through as if it will 100% will happen and be functioning by their enrollment.

- **DRESS CODE**: For major visits, institute a uniform dress code for coaches, select staff and interns. Whether it's khaki shorts and polos or dress shoes and slacks with a collared shirt, make everyone aware of dress code for the weekend or select events.

- **IMPROVEMENTS**: Reassess your campus tours each year and get feedback from those regularly involved on how you can streamline and improve your tours year-to-year. What works, what doesn't work?

SELLING PROGRAM: KEY PICTURES IN OFFICE

As you develop your recruiting picture library, pick the best to display in your office and facility. Develop a budget for having pictures updated annually within the facility or even more often after big wins or awards. Update pictures often to keep up-to-date with program accomplishments.

If the budget is tight, find ways to get these pictures, and to keep up with the new additions in a timely way. There are firms who specialize in displays but if you think hard enough you can come up with creative ways to display your success in a budget-friendly way. You can rotate large post prints from CVS or Kinko's, just invest in a nice frame.

If budget is available, install flat screens in those areas so pictures can be easily updated, rotated and changed throughout the year, or for highlight videos to loop.

WHEN CHOOSING GAME PICTURES, ALWAYS SELECT PICTURES FROM WINS—ESPECIALLY OVER RIVALS, RANKED TEAMS AND HOME GAMES. AFTER A BIG WIN—GET YOUR HANDS ON AS MANY PICTURES FROM THAT GAME THAT YOU CAN TO USE FOR OFFICE DISPLAYS, MAILOUTS AND SOCIAL MEDIA. YOU CAN'T HAVE TOO MANY FROM THESE GAMES, ESPECIALLY HOME GAMES!

Psychologically, you and your players will see these displays every day, and every day you will remember that you "can." Automatically update in a timely manner to be updated by important campus visits. Even when starting with small achievements, small steps that your program has taken can be used for these displays. You are always trying improve your program with milestones and achievements that have never been done before. These achievements should be celebrated – even when starting small. Wins over rivals, wins over ranked teams, wins at home—you can't get enough of these pictures. Work on eliminating doubts and insecurities, which are common even in the most successful coaches and players, and these every day visual reminders are good for program confidence and for helping recruits visualize your program's recent success and improvements.

Carefully select (and proactively gather) great recruiting gameday pictures, they'll provide great talking points when giving tours during Official and Unofficial Visits.

MAXIMIZE THE IMPACT THAT YOU CAN MAKE VISUALLY AROUND THE FACILITY. FIND WAYS TO RECREATE THE EXCITEMENT OF GAMEDAY AND BIG WINS!

When giving tours of your offices, weight room, training room or other areas of the facility, you have plenty of places to stop and relive the moment and excitement with your visitors. Make a list of spaces where these types of pictures can be added for stops along your walking tours.

Never display or use pictures for mailouts that show an empty crowd. Photoshop pictures to use as action pictures with no background, or blur background!

Don't leave this important responsibility to chance or someone else's choice... someone internally on YOUR staff needs to be in charge of this. Any and every milestone to your program needs to be blown up and visible to your prospects and seen daily by your players and staff!

Have "Walls of Fame" dedicated throughout the facility of current and former players – All-Americans, All-Conference, graduates, best strength and conditioning performers, team captains, conference players of the week and team players of the week. Your current players will love seeing themselves around the facility, and it gives prospects motivation to one day be one of your program's best to be honored on the "Wall of Fame."

SELLING PROGRAM: BE PREPARED TO ANSWER QUESTIONS

Players and parents are full of questions, here are some commonly-asked questions that you should be prepared to answer, or can proactively answer before they've even asked (as long as the answers are positive)!

#1: What are grad rates of your team and how do they compare nationally within your sport? How do grad rates compare to the schools that the recruit is looking at? Does your Athletic Department and your specific team graduate players? What percentage of your university teams' players have graduated in the last 5-10 years?

#2: What are the grad rates under your head coach? Has your staff and head coach made graduating players a priority to them over their career? What percentage of players have graduated in the last 5-10 years under the head coach, even if they were at other schools?

#3: Where exactly are you located? What's the distance to major attractions, metropolitan cities, recruiting hotbeds? Quickest ways to their hometown, if your campus is hard to access? Travel time by plane, bus or train?

#4: What does the town have to offer off-campus? Outdoor activities, beaches, concerts, shopping, other sports teams? What is popular, great and different about your city? Does your city rank on any great lifestyle lists or "Best Cities" lists?

#5: Are the other teams at your school successful within the conference and in post-season play? Is the Athletic Director and administration happy being competitive or are they able to provide all teams resources to win? Do most of the teams win on a consistent level?

#6: How many players, at that position, do you plan to sign in each graduating class? How many players, at each position, have already committed? How many slots are available by signing class?

#7: What is the average class size? Check the official Admissions information from the University for stats!

#8: What competitive advantages – in terms of resources and operating budget -- does the Athletic Department have? Are you providing the competitive resources needed to win consistently?

#9: What is the head coach's personality? Players often mimic their coaches, are they great people? Do you truly put players first in terms of lessons that they are teaching them and standards they are setting? What "family" atmosphere aspects of your program can you highlight?

#10: What is your plan for each top recruit? You can use a cookie-cutter plan and add or subtract minor details based on player preferences. Deep down, great players crave expectations and love a detailed plan of how you can help them achieve their goals!

MORE QUESTIONS THAT WILL BE ASKED DURING RECRUITING PROCESS...

ACADEMICS
– What percentage of classes have fewer than 25 students? Fewer than 50 students? What are the class sizes within the prospect's intended major?

– Do you offer a major that they are interested in? What majors does the University offer?

– Can the prospect sit in on a class during their visit, particularly in their desired major?

– What are the freshman year credit requirements? What will be their freshman year required classes?

– How diverse is the campus – students, professors and community?

– Will they need to enroll in summer school classes at any point and what is the Athletic Department's policy on summer school fees?

– Do athletes have required study hall hours? What is the team's policy on required study hall?

– What is a sample daily schedule during the season and in the off-season?

– Are tutors available?

- What technology resources are available to student-athletes?

– Does the Athletic Department or school help with networking or job fairs?

– Has the team or department had any academic scandals within recent years? If so, how have you addressed them?

– If applicable, are there special accommodations for students with learning disabilities? If so, what are they? What history do you have with students with learning disabilities?

– What are common majors that your athletes are enrolled in? What are your top student-athletes majoring in?

– If the recruit plans to go to grad school, law school or medical school—will they be in a program that will help them accomplish their future goals? Do you have a strong academic program nationally that interests them?

– Is the academic program a national leader? Is that something that is important to them or are they more interested in "hands on" opportunities with internships?

– If they are interested in internships, are you in the right city where they may be able to network and find these opportunities? What great internships can you place them in?

– Which major companies recruit students from that university? Fortune 500 companies? What are the biggest companies and employers in your city?

THE TOWN/UNIVERSITY COMMUNITY
– Universities are either in a "college town" or in big cities—will they be comfortable there? Some big-city players get bored easily in small towns or players from small towns are overwhelmed in big cities—do they like the community they will be living in? How can you spin it either way?

– What are the crime rates of the city? How safe is campus? What are the surrounding neighborhoods like?

– Are they interested in living in a new city outside of their comfort zone for a few years? Move to big city, move out of big city, major climate change, closer to other family/friends. Will they be moving to a city that they've always dreamed of living in?

– If they have a spouse and/or children—how will that play into their decision? Is distance a factor? Will they be moving with them? Can they talk to other players within the program that are also married or are parents and see how they are able to manage the transition? Do you offer campus family housing?

ATHLETIC DEPARTMENT
– Does the Athletic Department have great leadership from the Athletic Director and what is the University President's involvement in Athletics?

– Is the department improving and always bringing in more resources and improvements? What new facilities, technology, new athletic training treatments can you highlight?

– Are your players respected in the community as positive role models? Do they have a history with legal issues- how will you address player arrests?

– Is the Athletic Department profiting? What is your operating budget and how does it compare to the other schools that they are looking at?

YOUR TEAM
– Are you a team on the rise?

– Will they have time to develop or will they be thrown into the fire as a freshman? Are they expected to deliver right away and carry the team? Is there a strong foundation of quality players already in the system that they can learn from and win with? Are you starting from scratch or are there great pieces already in place? You can spin either way: "We're looking for a player just like you with great leadership to take us there," or market as a situation that they can step into and develop quickly with great mentors leading them.

– What is the record of success of the program in last 5-10 years? If the coaching staff is new, what is your track record of success at previous schools? What winning experience does the staff have?

– How much experience does the staff have combined? Has a majority of the staff worked together for several years under the head coach or are coaches constantly coming and going? Promote staff continuity!

– Does the team have the opportunity to be a major upset team? Does that excite your recruits? Do you play with exceptional heart and feed off of the underdog role?

– If you are a major football or basketball Division I program, does the team charter flights for most road games so that players miss less class time? Do you bring tutors or academic counselors on the road?

– Are there certain traditions that are beloved by the fanbase that excites the prospect?

– What are the dining halls like? Do you have nutritionists who will help them with nutrition, vitamins, supplements, off-campus cooking/meal planning, weight gain plans?

– Are your games televised so that their friends and family can watch often?

- What strength and conditioning improvements can they expect to make in the first year? In the second year? Show before and after pictures of your current starters to show how far they've come physically under your direction.

– What is the path for your team to play for a championship or major post-season opportunity?

- Do they want to be a part of a major regional or national rivalry game?

- What does the conference offer in terms of academic prestige, competition, tradition, exposure?

- Do the students show up for games? Is there good attendance at games?

- Is the stadium close to campus? Is it a place they've always dreamed of playing? Does it have a nickname? What do media or opponents have to say about your gameday atmosphere?

- Is your team disciplined on-the-field or do they make stupid mistakes? Is your team disciplined off-the field with no arrests, suspensions or scandals?

- Are your players accountable to each other and competitive? Do they have a positive attitude, work ethic and desire to get better?

- Can they help recruit a 'super class' of other recruits who can come in and make a difference, especially as an underdog team?

SELLING PROGRAM: LEADERSHIP DEVELOPMENT AND COMMUNITY SERVICE

Great leaders are attracted to other great leaders. Great players want to play with other great players.

Leadership isn't natural to a lot of players, it's something that needs to be developed and drawn out. Leadership can turn a naturally-talented player into a champion. A lot of players know they're in a leadership position but don't necessarily know how to grow into a leader. Many athletes are afraid to speak up in front of the group, especially as freshmen or sophomores.

Attract players who are natural-born leaders, or talented players who look to expand their role as a leader, and who know it's an attribute that can help them improve. As prep players, have conversations with your recruits now as to how they can provide more leadership for their team. Help them build that skill now and develop that connection with them. Help them develop their leadership in their own individual way, there is no "right" way to lead!

Community service brings value to your players lives – they are a part of something bigger than themselves. They feel their impact in the community, and can go home at night and appreciate their unlimited meal plan, tons of free gear, a roof over the heads (in a building full of friends), financial assistance towards a college degree and more opportunities in front of them than the average person.

Create a Leadership Panel, hold leadership development activities, invite great leadership speakers to your program and publicize this to your prospects. Emphasize your pride in the leadership of your current players and voice this to your prospects! Have them look to you as someone who can help them grow their leadership skills.

Along with skill development, leadership development is one of the greatest assets that you can have in your recruiting arsenal. Helping players develop this skill will bond you with your top recruits. As your players interact in leadership and community projects, be sure to gather pictures from these experiences for future recruiting use.

SELLING PROGRAM: ATTENDANCE

As you are building your program and drawing the community and student body in, look for small wins in terms of attendance. Sellouts, capacity crowds, records-broken, conference attendance records all take time and are major accomplishments – recognize them all and make a big deal of them! Have your entire staff put time and effort into ways to increase attendance!

Before each game tweet your excitement about the student sections being involved, telling your fanbase that you need them and need them loud. Give pre-game shoutouts to the band, cheerleaders and student groups. Post a pre-game image on Facebook, Instagram and Twitter with time, location, opponent and TV/Radio coverage. Hype up each game on social media, as creatively and energetically as possible! Shoutout your fans and students – inviting them to games, as genuinely as possible!

Emphasize and publicize the excitement around your program with the community – increases in season tickets, increases in renewals, students in line for rival games, student camping out... build the buzz about the excitement surrounding your program, celebrate it and publicize it!

After games, even after losses, send out your thanks to the fans, university, community and students. Just as you put your heart and energy into the game—they did too. Take time to appreciate them and acknowledge their efforts.

If playing in front of empty stands, edit pictures of players that you use for recruiting mailouts, social media or your team website to limit publicizing empty seats. Cut out or blur the background to cover up the empty stands issue. It's better to not have a picture than to have one with your players playing in front of an empty home stadium or arena – find creative ways to disguise this recruiting obstacle!

SELLING PROGRAM: CELEBRATIONS

As a coach, you direct your players to practice a lot of things—one thing not to overlook is practicing your post-game celebrations, your bench/sideline responsibilities, your substitutions and your celebrations after scores or big plays.

It may sound silly, but it's not an aspect to overlook. Your celebrations are a reflection of your team to your fanbase, your recruits and your university.

- **BENCH**: They're there to supply the energy, the positivity and to help set the pulse of the game. Detail their responsibility during the game, to keep the energy and faith from pre-game warmups to the final buzzer. Redshirt players, injured players, backups, grad assistants and managers are all responsible for bench energy on gameday.

- **SCORES/BIG PLAYS**: Direct your players to ALWAYS huddle together to celebrate scores or big plays as a TEAM. It's not just two or three players high-fiving, it's the entire lineup. Detail them on celebrating as a team, and their actions with the refs. Take time to express what is expected and what isn't allowed.

- **POST-GAME**: Win or lose, develop a tradition for your players and coaches to interact with fans: sing the Alma Mater together, post-game autograph sessions, celebrations with the student section, interacting with the band and cheerleaders. Whether they were a player, fan, cheerleader or member of the band – they were investing their time. Celebrate together.

- **SUBSTITUTIONS**: Have a staffer responsible for substitutes and ensuring that you have the proper number of players on the field or court. Develop a system. Include a high-five or passing of a towel in these interactions.

HAVE GRAD ASSISTANTS, STRENGTH COACHES OR ASSISTANT COACHES RESPONSIBLE FOR KEEPING UP WITH BENCH ENERGY, CELEBRATIONS, POST-GAME TRADITIONS AND SUBSTITUTIONS ON GAMEDAY. YOUR CELEBRATIONS ARE A REFLECTION OF YOUR TEAM TO YOUR FANBASE, YOUR RECRUITS AND YOUR UNIVERSITY.

SELLING PROGRAM: GOLD STAR PLAYERS
As you detail your goals and expectations to your players, both on and off-the-field, you need to reward those who meet and exceed those high standards.

As children are prideful in having their latest project up on the fridge, you might be surprised how motivating or culture-changing it can be for your college-aged students too.

Encourage everyone to aim to be a part of this exclusive group—give it a catchy name.

Precisely outline expectations for your key periods throughout the year, depending on your sport—quarters, semesters, season, off-season, non-conference season, conference season, summer school. However you choose to break up the year, precisely detail your expectations with attendance, GPA, practice and game goals for each period. Each period can have its own specific achievement requirements.

Those players who meet your achievement requirements, which may be a small percentage when taking over a program: publically identify them! Applaud them in front of their teammates and the fanbase, and encourage the rest of the roster to get on board!

Speak with your Compliance Office to get approval to award this group a quarterly t-shirt, meal or prize. A tangible reward will drive your players, believe it or not. Give them shoutouts on social media, in press conferences and on the program's website. Let them have a tangible reward (with Compliance's approval) for members who have earned extra privileges or rewards over the quarter or semester.

Take pride with this group. Make it an exclusive clique that others want to be a part of. It may start small, only a few players may qualify when you take over a losing program. Don't lower the bar so that everyone is a part of it – make membership have great value, accomplishment and pride. Over time, the more members this group has, the more likely your chances are to develop a winning program.

ATHLETES ARE EXTREMELY GOAL-DRIVEN, YOU NEED TO TAP INTO THIS MORE THAN JUST ON GAMEDAYS! TAP INTO THIS COMPETITIVE DAILY SPIRIT IN THE OFF-SEASON, IN THE SUMMER AND WITH OFF-THE-FIELD ACHIEVEMENTS. PLAYERS NEED BLACK AND WHITE EXPECTATIONS AND GOALS – DETAIL WHAT YOUR EXPECTATIONS ARE FOR A CHAMPIONSHIP-CALIBER TEAM AND REWARD THOSE WHO ACHIEVE THESE EXPECTATIONS!

SELLING PROGRAM: LEGENDS OF PROGRAMS
Identify a list of your university's outstanding former players, especially recent players.
- Best players position-by-position
- National or Conference Award winners
- Current or past pro players
- Players who are successful in business or career
- Former players who held campus leadership positions
- Academic standouts

If your sport has few standouts, can you research a similar list of standouts from any of your university's sports or outstanding graduates?

SELLING PROGRAM: CAMPUS SAFETY
In terms of campus safety, perception is reality. Campus and community safety is a common and major concern for parents, and a top reason why programs are eliminated. Get your facts straight, and be prepared for the fact that you may never be able to change the perception of your community to some parents if you are located in a metropolitan city!

I've worked in tiny college towns, mid-sized college towns and in global metropolitan cities and truthfully their safety factors were very similar. Dangerous neighborhoods within a mile or less are near every campus!

College students can find trouble anywhere—if they want something, they'll find it. No campus is safe from predators, violence, drugs or guns. No campus is truly "safe."

Perception is reality: if parents feel the city is too dangerous, you might not be able to overcome this factor. Find city records and statistics and compare them to other cities and campuses that your prospects are looking at.

You may need to shift your focus to prospects who are from similar cities who are used to big-city life.

SELLING PROGRAM: NEGATIVE RECRUITING

Career-wise, it's not a good philosophy to talk trash about other programs or coaches. Sure, a lot of coaches plant seeds of doubt or mistrust, and other coaches outright trash talk rival coaches and programs, but in the end, does it really work?

Instead, focus on marketing your program and what you can DO for players. A more tactful way is to breakdown actual FACTS, show factually how your program compares (and stands out) versus your rivals or even better, versus programs that your top prospects are considering.

HIGHLIGHT YOUR POSITIVES INSTEAD OF CONSTANTLY POINTING OUT YOUR OPPONENTS NEGATIVES! FIGHT BACK WITH ALL THE POSITIVES THAT YOU HAVE TO OFFER!

Bad-mouthing other coaches gets back to them, and in the big picture of building your personal career, it's best not to make enemies in the profession. You may be trying to make your current school look better in the short run by ripping another program, but in the long run, you are making enemies with coaches who could possibly hire you down the road.

Like kids caught in the middle of divorcing parents, recruits can see through the name-calling and trash talking. Recruits and their parents need to respect you and your program in order to choose you, and playing into negative recruiting isn't a good look.

SELLING PROGRAM: RESPONDING TO CORRESPONDENCE
If possible, you need to develop a system to respond to all correspondence. If financially tight, find a way to use email templates and online questionnaires to respond.

All phone calls, emails, letters and videos should receive a response. Responses fall into one of three categories:

- NOT INTERESTED: Thank you for your interest. Good luck this season. Camp info. Send a questionnaire that is coded for "Not a prospect" or email a link to your generic questionnaire.

- RESEARCH FURTHER: Send a coded questionnaire and request video. Look online for video. Call prep coaches or contacts in the region.

- BEGIN RECRUITMENT: Love what you see? Immediately add to the database, send initial package, add to mailing list and send a coded questionnaire.

As you respond to unsolicited correspondence, keep a running Excel file of email addresses and mailing addresses for camp mailouts. Once camp dates are set and registration is open, you have a good database of contacts to reach out to.

SELLING PROGRAM: GREAT VIDEO STAFF
An area of your program that needs quality attention, after bringing in a great coaching staff and strength staff, is a video staffer (or staffers or interns) who can help generate team motivational videos, who can organize and maintain your recruit video library and who can create short social media clips.

This generation of high school players grew up on YouTube, this is how they learn to do things, interact and where they find entertainment. Videos are essential for recruiting presentations, pre-game motivation during team meetings and to hype up and interact with fans on social media!

Put time, energy and budget towards finding the right person for this critical area!

If low on budget, be rich in creativity! Your campus is full of student workers or interns who want to build their resume.

CHAPTER #8
SELLING YOURSELF

"You can't build a reputation on what you are going to do."
-HENRY FORD

"Ability may get you to the top, but it takes character to keep you there."
-JOHN WOODEN

"Some of us will do our jobs well and some will not, but we will be judged by only one thing-the result."
-VINCE LOBARDI

"Every time you have to speak, you are auditioning for leadership."
-JAMES HUMES

SELLING YOURSELF: WINNING

Again, there is no truer statement than, "Winning cures everything," especially in recruiting.

Obviously, recruiting and winning go hand-in-hand. If you can win, getting in the door with high-quality prospects becomes much easier. Winning makes you instantly credible (although, this doesn't last season-to-season). Winning makes the decision easier for prospects and their families-- there's hard proof that you know what you're doing and can help them become successful. You're not selling a fairy tale, you're selling facts! Your calls will get answered more often when you're winning and trust is easier to build.

WINNING CURES EVERYTHING:
- Win versus ranked opponents!
- Win within the conference!
- Win in the post-season!
- Win the cupcake games, too!
- ... Just win, BABY!

As you need to need to streamline your time spent on recruiting to get the most out of every minute, you also need to be productive in your time spent on game preparations and player development. A revolving door of staff, university outreach, community outreach and boosters will be asking you to devote time to various events, issues and causes – you need to learn how to say 'no.'

You won't be able to make everyone happy who comes through your office door, not to mention your own kids, family and friends. To do YOUR job well, you won't have time to accept every invite or request that comes through your door. In a perfect world, you could do every PSA requested, make every community relations appearance, answer every fans request and watch every recruits video-- but you just don't have the time. If you are at a big-budget school, you may have staff to help you cover some of these requests. If you are like coaches at most schools, you won't, so you MUST prioritize and not get tied up with issues that won't help you win or sign top recruits!

> **GREAT COACHES KNOW THAT IN ORDER TO FOCUS THEIR TIME ON GAME AND PRACTICE PREPERATIONS YOU MUST LEARN TO SAY NO TO MANY OUTSIDE REQUESTS!**

SELLING YOURSELF: DEVELOP PLAYERS

One of the most effective ways to get players to buy into your vision is to have a track record as a coach who develops their position players. Even if you are at a low-profile school, being able to have solid numbers and improvements of your current players to show recruits helps "sell the dream." When trying to get prospects to buy into the dreams you have for your program, a great recruiting tool is your track record for helping players improve!

KEEP TRACK OF THE "BEFORE" AND "AFTER" OF YOUR PLAYERS: PHYSICAL MEASUREMENTS, WEIGHT GAINS AND LOSSES, STATISTICAL IMPROVEMENTS, IMPROVEMENTS IN THE WINS COLUMN, ACADEMIC IMPROVEMENTS. AS A STAFF, TAKE RESPONSIBILITY TO TRACK AND MAINTAIN THESE IMPROVEMENT RECORDS FOR EACH AREA OF YOUR PROGRAM.

If you have proven results on an individual player basis, you're not really selling a dream. Your team may not be winning championships yet, but you can earn some great leverage by showing concrete numbers, pictures and proof of improvements of your current and past players. Proof that you are on the right track and are just trying to recruit the "missing pieces."

When you have a proven record of success, players buy in quicker. Players won't fight discipline as much if they believe following your instructions can lead them to where they want to be. You won't waste months or a year trying to get them to take coaching or to buy in. When you have proven that you can win or develop players to a high level of success, they will follow your direction!

WHEN TRYING TO SELL YOUR VISION IT'S A LOT MORE BELIEVABLE AND CREDIBLE WHEN YOU HAVE A PROVEN BACKGROUND OF BEING A GREAT COACH WHOSE PLAYERS IMPROVE.

WHY PLAYER FUNDAMENTALS DON'T IMPROVE:
- Player resists coaching
- Player will not work at tempo required to improve
- Player does not possesses innate athletic ability
- Not enough repetition
- Poor teaching

- Prepare your position players with a sense of urgency, never take a laid-back approach to the game, always work up-tempo with them.

- Work to have a team that polices itself from within, players that hold each other accountable. Identify your leaders and build them even higher. Work to bring players into your program that are deeply committed to improving. Eliminate players who are selfish and don't buy into your philosophy.

- Correct mistakes, express the value of players investing extra time and effort into their craft. If their behaviors or results are average or below, don't reward. Reward only excellent effort and results, don't dilute the power of reward and motivation.

- When dealing with issues, deal with players one-on-one and behind closed doors. Don't gossip about players with or in front of other players. Don't try to correct negative behaviors in front of the media, or blame players individually during press conferences.

- Help your players develop, and develop them as leaders by instilling a mentorship program. As they develop, help them develop others!

- Your current players will be ambassadors during recruiting, and they'll tell it like it is. You may be recruiting prospects from their former high school or town, and they'll be giving their frank opinions when asked.

SELLING YOURSELF: SIMPLE, PROVEN STRATEGY

Another common trait that great coaches have in common: they have their own simple, proven strategy on gameday and they believe in their plan.

No great head coach enters the season saying, "We're going to go out and win a bunch of games." Instead, they have a very specific, strategic core set of team goals—both season and game goals.

All great head coaches tend to focus on 4-5 key game statistics and intangibles, knowing that the odds are in their favor if their team can do X, Y and Z.

TO SELL, YOU NEED A PLAN. YOU NEED A DETAILED VISION FOR PROSPECTS TO BUY IN TO.

As you develop your winning formula, even as a position coach, you need to develop your simple, proven strategy to detail to recruits. You need to get your current players to focus on a few key fundamentals, excel at those and articulate this to your recruits. If we can do X, Y and Z, we will be in a great position to accomplish all of our goals.

To sell, you need a plan. You need a detailed vision for prospects to buy in to. Recruits want leadership, direction, and a simple, proven plan is a good way to leverage your program and its ability to develop players.

Like mission statements, proven plans are crystal clear for current players and are often distributed to recruits during the recruiting process.

Again, as a recruiter you will often be "selling a dream." We're going to go out and win championships, graduate players and put you in a great position after graduation. Well, you need to detail HOW. HOW are you going to win games? Write your simple strategy down, plaster around the facility and distribute to your players and recruits in crystal clear verbiage, exactly how you will do that. Break it down as simply as possible, in stages if necessary.

NEVER SETTLE FOR PAST ACHIEVEMENTS.
ALWAYS BE PLANNING FOR YOUR NEXT BIG ACCOMPLISHMENT.

SELLING YOURSELF: ANALYTICS
Data is priceless, prospects want to see concrete evidence: What can you and your staff do to help them improve? How have your players improved over your career? How have your current players improved from their freshman year?

Research and only promote good or great numbers: use +/- data or percentages, whichever sounds better...

EXAMPLES:
Individual stats: Which key stats have your current or recent players improved on?
• Johnny Basketball improved from 25.5% to 31.7% from freshman year to sophomore year
• Football improved his yards per carry from 4.5 to 6.4 from last year

Weight Room: Include before and after pictures with their measurements compared year-to-year
• Michael Football dropped his 40-yard dash from a 4.9 to a 4.7.
• Thomas Basketball increased his bench from 200 to 260.

Team stats: How have you improved the team overall? Wins, accuracy, team defense/offense, etc.
• Team defense improved from 360 yards/game to 333 yards/game
• Team turnovers improved from 11/game to 9/game.

Academics: How have academic numbers improved? Overall team GPA, number of players over 3.0 GPA.
• Our Team GPA increased from a 2.8 in the Fall to a 3.2 in the Spring
• 85% of our team carries a 3.0 cumulative GPA or higher entering this semester.

Opportunities: Playing Time or Stats by Position
• An average of 45 points/game scored by our guards is graduating this semester.
• An average of 38 minutes/game by our guards are graduating this semester.

SELLING YOURSELF: GENUINE PERSONALITY

A championship team is made up of puzzle pieces of different personalities, and it's okay for there to be unique personas and personal strengths throughout the staff. What's more important than conforming personalities, is that everyone is working towards the same GOALS.

Fake and phony is sniffed out by high school and college kids-- quick. Recruiting-wise, it's always better to be yourself than to act like someone you're not. You don't have to act 20 or 30 years younger, or speak the latest slang. You don't have to pretend to be the nicest, most polite person on the planet-- kids will see right through you. And so will their parents. And if they feel that you aren't being real with them, they won't trust you. And if they don't trust you, you're wasting your time!

Some coaches are nerdy but technical geniuses. Some coaches have no personality but are tremendous at every other aspect of the job-- consider lightening their recruiting responsibilities. I've been on staffs where a coach or two didn't go out on the road unless to evaluate players just because their personalities didn't mesh with recruits. Not everyone has "it." On the other hand, I've worked with coaches who may not have had the best results on the field, but they could sign a high percentage of prospects for the program. For some coaches, their recruiting abilities helped them keep their job!

THE BEST RECRUITERS CAN TALK TO ANYONE AT ANY TIME ABOUT ANYTHING. THEY CAN BLEND INTO ANY SITUATION, WALK INTO HOME VISITS OR GYMS FROM THE HAMPTONS TO LITTLE HAITI TO THE RANCHES OF TEXAS TO THE WOODS OF WEST VIRGINIA TO COMPTON TO MALIBU TO CHICAGO TO SAMOA AND BLEND IN LIKE THE FAVORITE COUSIN. NOT EVERYONE HAS THAT SKILL, BUT THOSE WHO DO WILL SUCCEED GREATLY IN THE RECRUITING GAME.

For some of you, your personality and ability to recruit will be your biggest career strength. Your ability to SIGN top players will help you get and keep jobs, when sometimes you aren't carrying the load on gameday. For others, you can learn to improve your recruiting skills and luckily that starts with just being who you are.

SELLING YOURSELF: QUALITIES OF SUCCESSFUL COACHES

- They demand perfection in everything that their players do, even off-the-field

- They understand that winning is the only thing that they will be judged on and can balance game preparations, strategy and player development with other job requirements that don't necessarily affect wins and losses

- They learn from every coach they have worked for, and keep great notes and files of info that have been passed down to them!

- They are great communicators

- They aren't caught off guard

- They demand discipline & are building a team that can be disciplined from within

- They can win versus ranked opponents

- Their teams fight back when down

- They know how to motivate their players and are trusted by their team

- They have faith and passion in their plan, staff and players

- They know how to move on after losses and setbacks

- Their players are accountable

- They are great teachers and are able to simplify the gameplan

- They demand their players respect program and honor of being a college athlete

- Their practices are tough

- They have strong relationships with other coaches across the sport at every level (high school, college and pros)

- They expect their players to graduate

- They are prepared for the next step

- They enjoy the process

- They know how to manage a staff

- They attack issues head on

SELLING YOURSELF: QUALITIES OF SUCCESSFUL RECRUITERS

Coaching and recruiting are two completely different jobs-- not many people understand that! Recruiting and coaching require two different skill sets. Just because you are a great recruiter, that doesn't necessarily mean that you are a great coach. And there are really great X's and O's coaches out there who aren't naturally great recruiters.

Characteristics of great recruiters include:

- A genuine personality

- A master of marketing – 24/7/365

- A high-level of organization and attention to detail

- A coach who is diligent in their work ethic

- The ability to put on a show in order to market their program

- The ability to get to know who or what is important in each prospect's life and to keep up with what is going on in their world

- The ability to create a parental role in their recruits' life and current player's life

- The effort of getting to know all of the decision makers and influencers in each prospects life

- A confidence about their program, what they can offer players and the ability to get players to commit

- The ability to be able to move on to the next player if they aren't getting feedback or interest from their top choices

- Putting together an Official Visit weekend that will be a home run from each recruits' perspective, creating a vision that the prospect has told them that they are looking for in a program

- The ability to do talent and skill evaluations without solely relying on rankings or scouting reports

- The ability to determine position needs for the team and sign the best available player

- Having strong relationships with coaches and programs in regional areas that date back decades

SELLING YOURSELF: 3 WAYS YOU WANT TO BE THOUGHT OF

Put thought into your long-term career vision, what type of coach do you want to be? As you develop ways that you want your team to be perceived, also develop adjectives that you would like to be perceived as. Narrow those visions down to your top three characteristics. These are the three traits that you will speak of yourself, try to stick to these three main characteristics.

Remember, your audiences will mirror back to you what you put out there. As you look to develop these characteristics, remember that you can only "market" yourself for so long—you quickly need to begin walking the walk.

HOW DO YOU WANT TO BE PERCEIVED AS A COACH?:
- I care about my players as a whole: athletically, socially, spiritually
- I expect nothing but the best of my players
- Nobody will outwork me or my players
- I treat my players as if they were my own children
- My players are prepared for life after college
- I will never make an excuse
- I expect greatness from everyone in our program
- I put my players in great positions to win

Similar to how you will influence the way others think of your team (page 124), you can influence how others describe you. But remember—you must put in the work to back it up!

In phone calls with prospects at Coaching Clinics, media interviews, on social media—reinforce the three characteristics that you feel best describe you.

Slowly but surely, your audiences will mirror these adjectives back to you and begin perceiving you in these ways. If you have aspirations of becoming a head coach, begin this habit as an assistant.

SELLING YOURSELF: ENERGY

Your energy draws people in—you draw in what you put out there! You are responsible for the energy that you put in the universe, so the type of recruits that you draw in will be similar to your daily attitude.

Especially when recruiting or around your players, you have to bring tremendous attitude. Just got a speeding ticket, just got dumped, just had a fight with a friend—fake it. Clear your mind temporarily, put on a smile and carry yourself as if you're enthusiastically attacking the day.

If you want relentless, focused, mentally tough players then you must learn to shut out all of your personal negativity and be energetic and enthusiastic around your team.

SELLING PROGRAM: DO SOMETHING NEVER DONE BEFORE
Help your players do something that's never been done before. Even if you're starting with small accomplishments, focus on the steps that you will take to get them to their ultimate goals. Bigger accomplishments will come after you begin achieving smaller, more manageable goals. One of the first steps in changing the culture at a new program is to help your players build confidence and understand that the way they were preparing was not effective.

As a coach keep a running list of "firsts" or "improvements" that your position group or players are making. As a marketer, you need a running list of steps that your players are taking in the right direction. Programs and players don't develop overnight, although you may feel the pressure. Put together well thought-out steps and goals for your players to achieve over the next month, three months, six months and year.

SELLING YOURSELF: KEEP EVERYTHING
A unique characteristic among great coaches is that they are coaching packrats—they keep every game plan, drill, practice schedule, bowl schedule, pre-season plan, self-scout, camp packet, team rulebook, budget, recruiting philosophy, workout manual, motivational quote and more! They all have binders and binders full of useful information. They find great resources and stick to the basics, they stick with what works!

Of all these great coaches that I've learned from, none of them were re-inventing the wheel. They were all great teachers, they were all confident in their plan, they had great mentors and they all held on to valuable information as they got their hands on it, sometimes for decades! At times they'd pull out a handout with logos from schools they were at decades ago and we'd retype and go!

As a coach- -an assistant or head coach—you will have a full plate 24/7, 365. A huge time-saver is to have a great head start with policies, procedures, schedules and best practices—a blueprint that you can put your own touch on. For a lot of responsibilities, you won't have to start from scratch, you can simply tweak to add your own spin!

ONE OF THE BIGGEST SIMILARITIES AMONG GREAT COACHES IS THEIR DIVERSE COLLECTION OF DATA!

For example, camps don't just involve check-in, drills and certificate handouts, they involve insurance, facility rentals, hiring additional coaches, coach background checks, parent waivers, team assignments, dining hall reservation, ordering of camp shirts and much more.

As you move on throughout your career, these resources provide a great reference to you! They can help you take care of responsibilities that you may not remember in detail (or even realize). When it comes time for you to be in charge of a particular responsibility, or in charge of an entire program, you have a head start!

SELLING YOURSELF: HELP OF SPOUSE

During Official/Unofficial Visit weekends and camps, a tool to add to your recruiting arsenal is to include your spouse in the circle. Recruits and parents are always looking to feel "at home" and in a "family" situation. If you think it would benefit, bring your spouse and children into the picture.

Coach your spouse on your program's key selling points-- academics, traditions, player-coach relationships and community life. They don't need to "sell" particularly hard, but it's impressive to parents if spouses know more about the program than just about wins and losses.

Remember-- relationships are the key to recruiting, so anything that you can do to add to that "fit right in, feel-at-home" vibe-- bring it! Your spouse might be able to add to the conversations with families and strengthen the relationship. The family will also feel like a priority if you go through the effort to include your family in their recruitment, it shows that their family and child is a high priority to you.

Encourage and invite your spouse and children to be an active part of the program and friendly with your current position players. Have your players over to the house for a home-cooked meal or holiday feast (a pre-approved occasional meal through your Compliance Office,) and have your family attend practice and team functions weekly or monthly. If you're trying to "sell" a family environment, you need to create one!

Speak with the Business or Compliance Office about rules or policies relating to spouse meals to determine if they are budgeted or allowed. Can you pay for out-of-pocket if you feel it's worth it?

And obviously, if there is tension or negativity in your relationship or your children are at an unruly stage, it's not always necessary to include them. Decide if it will help or distract during the visit.

SELLING YOURSELF: YOUR OFFICE

An overlooked aspect of recruit marketing is your office. While there are daily responsibilities much more critical than interior décor, your office can help say a lot about you. Recruits and their families are excited to visit and are sizing you up. There are things that your office can say about you that you won't have to say for yourself.

Most schools won't pay for your office decorations—picture frames and photo enlargements -- but these are cheap ways you can upgrade your "visual resume" in your office.

Let your office speak about you personally, what makes you human outside of coaching? Professionally, what are your most proud 2-3 coaching moments? Who were the top 2-3 players that you've coached, do you have pictures with them?

OFFICE PICTURE SUGGESTIONS:
- Family pictures
- Pictures of your kids
- Pictures of your spouse
- Pictures from big wins
- Championship team pictures
- Pictures of you as a player
- Pictures of you doing favorite off-field hobby
- Your diploma
- Vacation pictures
- Pictures of you with celebs
- Pictures with your current position players
- Graduation pictures with your recent past players

SELLING YOURSELF: QUOTES FROM OTHERS

Your Sports Information Director is a great source for these and can assist you to gather and create more. Can you get quotes about the program, facilities, style of play, commodore or your coaching staff from:

- Former Players
- Pro Coaches
- National, Regional, Local Media Members
- Opponent Coaches (pulled from media articles)

You can say all the positive things about yourself and your program but it's much more credible to hear it from others as well.

CHAPTER #9
PERSONALITIES

"Treat people as if they were what they ought to be, and you help them become what they are capable of being."
-J. WOLFGANG VON GOETHE

"Becoming a leader is synonymous with becoming yourself. It is precisely that simple and it is also that difficult."
-WARREN BENNIS

"Don't permit fear of failure to prevent effort; we are all imperfect and will fail on occasion but fear of failure is the greatest failure of all."
-JOHN WOODEN

"If you want to be trusted, be trustworthy."
-STEPHEN COVEY

PERSONALITIES: TEAM CHEMISTRY

As you put a plan together with recruiting and off-season training, always put quality attention into building and maintaining team chemistry. I've worked with multiple head coaches who had turned down great, top talent for our programs because those recruits would have negatively impacted our team chemistry and lockerroom.

What championships have taught me is that there is a very thin, millimeter difference between wins and losses and what separated those teams were strong team chemistry, 3-4 years spent playing together, an off-the-field genuine bond, a strong bench and a season or two of adversity. A 1-point loss at the final seconds was eventually overcome by a 1-point win at the buzzer the next year—but what had gone in that year was monumental. As a whole, it wasn't as if we felt our team was the most talented entering each season, actually far from it. We weren't more talented than the teams we faced, but I guarantee we were tighter.

BE SELECTIVE OF THE PERSONALITIES THAT YOU BRING INTO YOUR LOCKERROOM.

Recruit personalities that can mesh—players that aren't selfish, players who can see the value of TEAM over starting or achieving individual achievements. Reward players who are carrying themselves the "right" way, encourage the rest who are underachieving to jump on board or possibly find a new home. All behaviors shouldn't be tolerated equally. Publically acknowledge players doing the little things right (even walk-ons), speak up in front of your team about the behaviors you want to see more of.

Create a lockerroom where players want to hang out. Spend time with your position players and team in the lockerroom every day. Create an environment they can spend time in between classes. It takes time and effort for you to build a strong relationship with your players, and for your players to build that relationship off-the-field.

Create a team that prides itself in needing each other. In every championship season I've been a part of there were times when our offense carried us, or the defense carried us—a variety of players had game-winning plays. Create an environment where team success is the only thing that matters. You can't recruit selfish prospects and expect them to develop a team mentality overnight.

PERSONALITIES: RANGE OF STAFF PERSONALITIES

As staffs are built by position needs and geographic recruiting backgrounds, it's also a good idea to build a staff that has a variety of personality strengths that are relatable and influential to your players. When hiring coaches or staff, it's better to take your time to make the best hire. Don't rush the hiring process if you don't feel like you've found a great "fit" for your staff.

Great strengths for coaches to have fall into a few different categories, mix and match your hires to have a balance:

- **RELATABLE**: Coaches who were once in your player's shoes. Have a couple coaches on staff who would be a natural mentor or friend to your current players. They are relatable:
    - Similar in age (3-5 years older)
    - Coaches who played collegiately at similar level
    - Went through similar upbringings
    - Became a parent at a young age
    - Played at that university
    - Similar religious beliefs
    - From the same regions as your recruiting hotbeds

- **HIGH-ENERGY**: A burst of human caffeine, coaches who are spirited, energetic and challenging.

- **DISCIPLINARIAN** – Coaches who players don't want to let down.

- **X's & O's**: They have a tremendous resume of producing great players and they know how to win!
    - Top nationally at teaching their position
    - Excellent strategists, students of the game, number crunchers
    - Have been part of successful staffs that have won conference or national championships
    - Were tremendous college players

- **SCOUTS**: Excellent at studying and analyzing opponents. Your players trust that they will be prepared and put in great positions to win verses any opponent.

- **CHEMISTRY-BUILDERS**: Coaches who have a pulse on team chemistry and energy. They keep the team loose- not too tight in stressful situations.

- **GENERATIONAL DIFFERENCES**: The entire college experience is a learning process, and many great lessons can be learned from coaches of another generation. From my experience, some of the strongest bonds were between players and coaches who were decades apart in age.

- <u>**GOOD WITH PARENTS**</u>: Having "it" with recruiting depends on your ability to connect with parents. Not everyone is able to mesh or relate to parents and all of their questions—be sure to have a few coaches on staff who are excellent with parents.

- <u>**HARD WORKERS**</u>: Your players need to see that hard work pays off, it's motivating to have extremely diligent and persistent staffers.

- <u>**FAMILY-ORIENTED**</u>: Coaches who have genuine respect for their family life. They take pride and an active role in being a spouse and parent.

PERSONALITIES: ADMIT MISTAKES

I've been a part of some of the top staffs in the country, and worked with some of the best athletes in America. Nobody is perfect, most have their insecurities and weaknesses. One of the biggest lessons that I've learned over the years, a consistent trait among successful competitors:

CHAMPIONS CAN ADMIT THEIR MISTAKES. INSTEAD OF PLACING BLAME ON SOMEONE OR SOMETHING ELSE, THEY FOCUS ON FIXING THEIR PROGRAM'S PROBLEMS. WHEN ERRORS INVOLVES OTHER PEOPLE, OR YOU FEEL THE URGE TO SAY, "I THINK SO-AND-SO MESSED UP THE...." – STOP, TAKE RESPONSIBILITY INSTEAD AND OUTLINE A SOLUTION.

A mentor I learned a lot from was first to say, "Hey, my bad. I messed up. This is what we're going to do..." and he'd lay out a quick resolution. He didn't point fingers, sweep his mistakes under the rug or ignore issues—he pointed them out, took responsibility, came up with a solution and moved on. The result? Everyone on our team felt comfortable admitting their errors. We weren't scared he'd find out and fire us. In fact, we felt comfortable enough to go to him with the problem and we'd quickly get it resolved.

In other organizations I've worked, employees would try to sweep their errors under the rug, where they would continue to grow and fester and potentially become a major problem. In those situations, coworkers learned to blame each other for errors to avoid personal responsibility, creating hostile environments.

AN ENVIRONMENT WHERE EVERYONE IS AFRAID TO MAKE MISTAKES IS AN ENVIRONMENT WHERE NO GROWTH HAPPENS. THE MOST SUCCESSFUL TEAMS AREN'T PARALYZED IN FEAR OF MAKING MISTAKES—AND THAT ATTITUDE MUST COME FROM THE TOP.

But, under this leader, we weren't apologizing for every tiny hiccup, but addressing actual problems or mix-ups and moving on quickly. You don't need to send a company-wide apology email or constantly throw yourself under the bus, but create an environment where problems can be addressed as they come up, corrected and left in the dust.

Employees become better at their job if they aren't always paranoid about making a mistake. You're going to make mistakes, but learning how to limit them and how to bounce back from them will be a difference-maker in your career.

Learn how to take responsibility in this type of environment, it trickles down to the field and your players. If players prepare and practice with this attitude of taking responsibility, they will become better players and you will eventually have a stronger team. Your players will see the importance of taking responsibility for their actions, become mature enough to admit an error and take ownership of their mistakes.

PERSONALITIES: DON'T BE CAUGHT OFF GUARD

Keep a detailed calendar year-to-year that you can roll over, not only to remember your upcoming appointments but to be able to look back on previous years to prepare for off-the-field responsibilities or projects.

Great coaches anticipate and prepare for what's next, they're managing current schedules and getting ahead for next week and next month!

Year-to-year the same events and responsibilities pop up. On each staff there are coaches who are prepared for responsibilities before even asked by the head coach, they're always ready for what's next. Then there are other assistants who run around like a chicken with their head cut off trying to handle requests from the head coach. The difference: certain assistant coaches anticipate what's next while others are caught off guard.

If you are working for the same head coach year-to-year or have worked for multiple schools, this will be a tremendous resource for you to look back on and develop into a great guide for your preparations. Each month, look back at which events, assignments and issues came up at the same time during the previous year, and get ahead on what is likely to be expected of you this year.

YOU WANT TO BE PREPARED FOR RESPONSIBILITIES BEFORE THEY COME UP, BEFORE YOU ARE EVEN ASKED OR ASSIGNED.

<u>**BUILD A CALENDAR THAT INCLUDES:**</u>
- Key Recruiting NCAA Periods: Evaluation Periods, Dead Periods
- Projects Assigned by Head Coach
- Recruiting Weekends (Official/Unofficial Visits and In-Home Visits)
- Player Workout Schedules (Off-season/Winter/Spring/Summer School)
- Holidays
- Family Birthdays and Anniversaries

- Team Banquets
- Pro days
- Major Recruiting Tournaments and Events
- Staff Retreats
- University Academic Dates (Drop/Add Deadline, Registration Periods, First Day of Class, Reading Days, Final Exams, Summer School Dates)
- Walk-on Tryouts
- Pre-season/Post-season Player Meetings
- Conference Head Coach Meetings
- Freshmen Orientation Dates
- Camps and Clinics
- Junior Days
- Athletic Department Hall of Fame Banquets
- Coaching Conventions
- Speaking Engagements
- Conference Championships
- Coaches Clinic

PERSONALITIES: NEVER BRING A BAD DAY TO THE OFFICE

If you expect your players to check most of their personal issues at the door before meetings and practice, you must do so as well! No matter what is going on in your personal life, or your insecurities about your program or team, you must be 110% passionate, energetic and positive at practice and in the office. If you're a head coach, your players and staff are mirroring you—copying your attitude and the way that you attack each day.

If you are a rude, bitter jerk you will have a team full of rude, bitter jerks. If you are mentally tough, positive, passionate and energetic under every circumstance—you will eventually have a relentless, unstoppable team that prepares and plays with the same characteristics!

Manage your family life, address major personal issues—seek counseling, exercise, manage stress, stay healthy, live a balanced life, have the right people around you—do WHATEVER you need to do to keep your outside life as managed and happy as possible.

Yes, there will be personal sickness, heartache, injustices, disagreements, divorces and drama in your home life. But, YOU set the attitude of your team and position group each day.

MANAGE STRESS:
- Exercise
- Eat well: On the road, on campus, with team
- Seek counseling
- Get out of the office at lunch
- Ask for a day off if you are dealing with a serious issue
- Make time for your family to visit facility
- Find ways to be an active participant in your child's activities
- Date night with spouse

PERSONALITIES: CALM, COOL AND COLLECTED

Erratic doesn't win championships – confidence in your plan, a relentless work ethic and a well-prepared team do. But, that's not always to say that is the situation you will find yourself in, or that you will never feel the pressure from thousands of fans, or the scrutiny of the media... but take a deep breath and pull yourself together, especially in front of your players and other coaches.

Never let them see you sweat!

Behind closed doors, I've witnessed more than a fair share of internal meltdowns, coaches freaking out before pivotal games! But, for your player's sake, don't let them see you sweat. Don't let them see you crack, doubt, worry or flinch. Your players mirror your energy and mentality – if they sense you're stressed, they will only play tighter.

A prepared player never plays desperate. Consistently look for ways to become more efficient with your time so that you can put more and more time into your opponent scouting, game plan and practice plans. Eliminate the unnecessary- especially during the season—to focus on preparing your team!

PERSONALITIES: PERSONAL LIFE

Because of the amount of time you are spending with prospects and players, and the parent-figure role you'll be playing in their lives, know that your personal life will be less and less yours. And, your personal life – in these days of social media and camera phones – will be less and less private.

Even before camera phones and social media: good old Athletic Department gossip. People talk and rumors spread quickly! Be careful of how much of your personal life you share with coworkers, and how you interact with staff socially. Competition is intense for jobs and promotions, power and money is involved. Some Athletic Departments are more dramatic than a reality show!

As you would hope your players carry themselves in a mature way, and represent your program and university in a positive way... you need to hold yourself to the same standards. In a job that is based on trust, character and interacting with minors, you realistically are held to high standards by your employers, fans and parents.

Trust and respect can quickly be broken or lost if your personal life interferes with your career. It's hard for your players to take coaching, listen to you and respect your rules if you can't respect the rules yourself.

- Don't drink in establishments that you know your players frequent. If a player arrives to an establishment where you or they are drinking, leave.
- Call a cab if intoxicated. A DUI will cost you your job.
- Consider dating outside of work walls only.
- Don't date parents of your recruits or players.
- Stay off apps primarily used for hooking up or casual meetups.
- If you are married, don't have affairs. If your relationship isn't working out, get a divorce.
- Especially if you are new on staff or a grad assistant, don't drink to intoxication with other staffers. Enjoy a beer or two, but leave it at that.
- Don't have an inappropriate relationship with any student.
- As you warn your players to watch the company they keep, do so yourself!

CHAPTER #10
SUPPORT STAFF

"Rather than focusing on things and time, focus on preserving and enhancing relationships and on accomplishing results."
-STEPHEN COVEY

"I don't know if I practiced more than anybody, but I sure practiced enough. I still wonder if somebody - somewhere - was practicing more than me."
-LARRY BIRD

"The price of greatness is responsibility."
-WINSTON CHURCHILL

"One man cannot make a team."
-KAREEM ABDUL-JABBAR

SUPPORT STAFF: ADMINISTRATIVE ASSISTANTS, GRAD ASSISTANTS & INTERNS

In order for you to begin streamlining your time and attention to the core areas that need your attention, maximize your efforts by building a great support staff around you. Put time and attention into recruiting, training and motivating this group of administrative assistants, grad assistants and student interns. Delegating can help you multiply your efforts if you find the right people, it takes time and effort to put the right group together.

As a staff, have a designated intern coordinator, whether it's a Director of Operations or grad assistant who can help recruit, train and supervise a staff of recruiting and administrative interns who are available throughout the year. Possibly create a full-time internship for credit or part time paid or volunteer positions. While there is a good pool of potential interns, you must take the time to screen them and train them.

STARBUCKS SPENDS MORE MONEY ON TRAINING THAN ON ADVERTISING, TAKE THE TIME IN THE OFFSEASON TO TRAIN THE RIGHT ASSISTANTS!

As I worked as an assistant to several accomplished coaches, even three "National Coach of the Year," honorees my main goal was to take as many non-coaching responsibilities and projects off their plate as possible in order to allow them to spend more time on the phone with recruits, scouting opponents or preparing for practice. I wanted to make their job as stress-free as possible with all of the details that don't have to do with games and practice.

RESPONSIBILITIES FOR SUPPORT STAFF:
- Prospect and Prep Coach Databases: Updating contact info using social media, questionnaires and online questionnaires to collect data
- Marketing feel of offices and events
- Correspondence: Recruit mailouts, handwritten notes and envelopes, presentations, former players, e-blasts, social media interactions
- Travel: Planning, Business Office responsibilities, real-time adjustments to schedules, AAU/Club tournament schedule planning
- Compliance: Paperwork, clarity on rules for specific questions
- Gatekeeper: Screening calls and visitors to limit direct interactions with coaching staff
- Official and Unofficial Visits: Planning of appointments, logistics, travel, itineraries, moving prospects from one location to another, check-in and registration, extra assistance for issues that come up
- Ticket Requests: For recruiting and personal use
- Campus Liaison for specific contacts or groups
- A response system for all unsolicited correspondence: letters, videos, emails, etc.

- Researching current news on your established prospects- Newspaper articles, score updates from prep games, social media updates
- Camps and Clinics
- Graphic Design
- Keeping facility and offices presentable at all times
- Campus and facility tours for non-priority prospects
- Create composite season schedule of all of your prospects games

CHAPTER #11
ADVICE FOR HEAD COACHES

"If we hire people smaller than ourselves, we'll become a company of midgets. If we hire people bigger than we are we'll become a company of giants."
-DAVID OGILVY

"When most managers realize they've hired a turtle they have a tendency to defend their personal selection because their ego can't admit to mistakes."
-STEPHEN COVEY

"A true leader has confidence to stand alone, courage to make tough decisions & compassion to listen to needs of others."
-DOUGALAS MACARTHUR

"Effective leadership is not about making speeches or being liked; leadership is defined by results, not attributes."
-PETER F. DRUCKER

ADVICE TO BECOME A GREAT HEAD COACH

One of the most common questions I get is, "What makes a great head coach?" I've had the honor of learning from tremendous head coaches and extremely driven assistant coaches, some who've gone on to become head coaches of their own programs.

Four areas that ALL great head coaches have in common:
- Game Planning / Knowledge of Game
- On-Field Teaching / Player Development
- Recruiting / Signing Players
- Strong Management Decision-Making, with Both Staff and Players

Most assistant coaches are really only masters of one or two of the four categories. Over time, some developed strengths in the weaker categories and went on to become a head coach.

In my opinion, to become a head coach – especially a great head coach – you must master all four! You won't last or find success if you are weak in any of the four areas. They're all equally important!

**AND ULTIMATELY, THE FACTOR THAT SEPARATES GREAT COACHES FROM SUB-PAR COACHES IS THEIR ABILITY TO MANAGE THEIR STAFF AND THEIR ABILITY TO DISCIPLINE AND MANAGE THEIR TEAM.
WHEN YOU PUT A GROUP OF HIGHLY-COMPETITIVE AND TALENTED PEOPLE TOGETHER, YOU NEED A GREAT MANAGER TO KEEP THEM WORKING TOGETHER, MOTIVATED AND TO KEEP THEM TEAM-ORIENTED. IT'S THE TOUGHEST PART OF THE JOB, AND ONE ASPECT NOT EVERY HEAD COACH IS PREPARED FOR.**

Yes, when you watch a winning team you know that the coach must be a great X's and O's coach. And yes, that's an important trait of a head coach but equally important is their ability to manage people:

- Manage staff and player chemistry
- Keep staff and players focused on TEAM goals
- Keep staff involved, have them take responsibility for at least one major aspect of program
- Keep staff and players motivated
- Not afraid to discipline players or staff

YOU CAN'T JUST BRING A TALENTED GROUP TOGETHER AND EXPECT THEM TO GEL AND WORK TOGETHER SEAMLESSLY. YOU MUST LEARN TO MANAGE PERSONALITIES, EGOS, MOTIVATIONS, COMPETITIVENESS, PERSONAL AGENDAS AND ATTITUDES. YOU NEED THE PIECES TO WORK TOGETHER AS ONE IN ORDER TO BE SUCCESSFUL.

As you develop into a head coach or coordinator, or want to improve in your position, these are the four areas you must focus on improving!

ADVICE FOR HEAD COACHES: A 'NO' PERSON
The higher you rise in your career, the more value there is in having a trusted person (or handful of people) who aren't "yes" men (or women). Successful programs aren't built off of one person, they are built off an environment where creativity is flowing and teamwork takes precedence. Many of the great coaches I've worked for hand a handful of people they could ask for opinions when making decisions – whether schematically, with discipline issues, budget issues, hiring decisions.

Don't surround yourself with people who only agree with you and always tell you what you want to hear. You'll need trusted mentors or staff who can be open and honest with you.

Depending on your role, you will have the power to make most final decisions, and you should stick with your gut and learn to have confidence in your decisions. But, don't be so strong-willed and untrusting that you can't take input from trusted mentors and assistants. To succeed, you will need allies to help you bounce ideas off of, to tell you when you are making a mistake, to tell you about issues going on behind your back, and people who can be honest with you. Nobody is perfect, and you won't reach a high level on your own. It is not a weakness, it can be a strength.

You need people who can funnel information to you that could be detrimental to your program, if not dealt with. The longer it takes for these key red flags or issues to get to you, the more likely they are to disrupt your program.

ADVICE FOR HEAD COACHES: SELF-SCOUT
Annually sit down with your entire staff and evaluate their effectiveness and an overview of your whole operation. Can you add new aspects to your recruiting? Do you need to adjust your recruiting gameplan?

WHAT ARE YOU DOING RIGHT? – Evaluate why your top, most-wanted prospects chose you. How can you build in these areas?

WHAT ARE YOU DOING WRONG? – Why are your top, most-wanted prospects going elsewhere?

WHAT IS OUT OF YOUR CONTROL? – What factors are out of your hands, and how can you figure this out earlier in the process in order to effectively manage your time? What are the "negatives" about your program or University that you can't change? Learn to decide when you need to end recruitment of an athlete who has concerns in these areas.

WHAT AREAS CAN YOU IMPROVE? – What areas of your program need an upgrade? What are the most urgent needed upgrades? Can you fundraise for these areas?

WHAT REGIONS BRING YOU MOST SUCCESS? – Geographically, which cities or regions have produced the most successful players in your program over the last several years? How can you get even more involved in these regions? Can you build better relationships with prep coaches in these areas?

WHO IS YOUR BIGGEST COMPETITION? – Which rival programs and coaches are invading your main recruiting regions? Which schools are recruiting your "home turf" successfully? Why are they succeeding? What do they have to offer that you don't?

WHICH MEMBERS OF YOUR STAFF ARE MOST VALUABLE FOR RECRUITING? LEAST VALUABLE? Can responsibilities or regions be shifted next year? Who needs to improve their recruiting abilities? Who should take on additional responsibilities? How can your coaches become better recruiters?

HOW CAN YOU SEPARATE YOURSELF? What makes you better than the schools you compete against? What can you add to your program to differentiate yourself?

HOW WILLING ARE PROSPECTS TO LEAVE? How much time in neighboring states should you spend trying to pull prospects away? Are they willing to leave or do they mostly sign with in-state schools?

ADVICE FOR HEAD COACHES: STREAMLINE
From an operations standpoint, you need an extremely streamlined set of procedures. You are working with a handful of people over and over, filling out the same paperwork, receiving the same tidbits of information (prospect addresses, transcripts), booking rooms at the same hotels, eating at a handful of the same restaurants.

The biggest time-saver and stress-saver you can have in recruiting is to have every major repetitive detail streamlined. In the off-season, take a look at your recruiting operations and regular contacts, and set up meetings with them to plan for the year ahead.

Some coaches are overwhelmed and lose their minds trying to get ready for visits. You should have an organized system together as a staff, by a certain point. Year-to-year, you shouldn't be stressed out trying to plan visit logistics. Sit down with each department you work with to get ahead on procedures. Eliminate as many of the logistics speed bumps that you can during the off-season to give yourself more time to focus on your prospects! You don't want to be running around like a crazy person during important Official and Unofficial Visits, you want a relaxed and calm vibe.

Make appointments with as much lead time as possible with academic counselors, professors, strength coaches, university contacts. Your extra consideration and respect for their time goes a LONG way, don't expect to drop last-minute requests on them and get a good result.

Each Athletic Department and University have different policies regarding budgets, signatures, credit card procedures. What's allowed, what's not? What will be rejected (and not reimbursed)? What are the Business Office policies regarding recruiting?

Make friends, not enemies, along the way with internal university and athletic department staff. Make timely appointments, confirm and be on time when dealing with university staff. After visit weekends, send a handwritten thank you note, and if possible, an extra camp shirt, marketing giveaway, or gesture of thanks. Treat these people with gratitude, and it will help you when you need a big, last-minute favor.

CHAPTER #12
ADVICE FOR ASSISTANT COACHES

"The role of leadership is to transform the complex situation into small pieces and prioritize them."
-CARLOS GHOSN

"There are no office hours for leaders."
-CARDINAL J GIBBONS

"One of the tests of leadership is the ability to recognize a problem before it becomes an emergency."
-ARNOLD GLASOW

"Leadership is the capacity to translate vision into reality."
-WARREN G. BENNIS

ASSISTANT COACHES: MASTER YOUR POSITION

Many of the assistant coaches that I've worked with aspired to be a head coach or coordinator. Almost every single one of them, at times, had their eye on their next promotion or dream job. Understandably! We're in a goal-oriented, cut-throat business—OF COURSE we are all trying to move up.

Don't lose sign of this: the quickest way to move up is to succeed where you are right now. I repeat, the quickest way to move up is to succeed where you are right now! Succeed this year and develop a strong commitment to success in your CURRENT position now and in the next few years to come. The road to your dream job starts here—you preach it to your players: Be the best at your position. Do your job. We all play a role.

In the big picture of your team—are your position players and off-field responsibilities among the strengths of the team? You need to take great pride in your position players and off-field responsibilities. Let nothing slide!

BUILDING A STRONG POSITION GROUP, YOUR PLAYERS:

- Are dependable and consistent, on and off-the-field (if not, recruit some).

- Are masters of fundamentals. They aren't always trying to win the game on every play... but they use near-perfect technique and often win one-on-one situations.

- Make few mistakes. They may not always be the home-run hitter (yet) but they rarely turn the ball over or make mental errors.

- Are prepared for each opponent. From your scouting reports, they have an edge because they know what to expect, they know tendencies and attack opponent weaknesses.

- Are confident. Confidence is a product of being prepared, not just a product of raw talent. Help your players build confidence by helping them be the most prepared players on the field.

- Are level-headed in pressure situations. They won't lose their temper, throw punches. Once again, a lack of composure is often a product of being desperate. A prepared player never plays desperate.

- Are in good academic standing. They know how to take care of business on and off-the-field and won't jeopardize their eligibility. You take a consistent, active role in their academics.

- They're on time and have no or few off-field issues. They are accountable. They are on time for weights, have no issues with equipment room and they show up for media responsibilities. They handle their business on every level!

- As a unit, your players are a strength of the team. Your position comes through in tough times, can rally, are tough and will never be a weakness that your opponents can attack.

- Are leaders. Your unit is a group who can be responsible when coaches aren't around, leaders in the weightroom, leaders in the lockerroom, leaders on campus and are a unit that can be depended on when the game is on the line.

- Are friends. They like each other and spend time together outside of the facility. Winning cannot occur without trust, and trust begins once your unit develops chemistry.

- Take pride in their role, no matter how small. They take pride in contributing to the success of the team, they take pride in being dependable and take pride in their work ethic and winning.

- Develop into a family. When your unit begins to play on a high level and the team begins to win—your unit will develop a brotherhood or sisterhood. They aren't just teammates, they're family.

- Consistently improve—from semester to semester, from year-to-year... your players are getting better. They master fundamentals. They get faster, bigger, stronger, smarter and more successful. There are concrete numbers to show these improvements.

- Can support other units when they are down. There is nothing like having the support and confidence from teammates when going through injuries, losing streaks or setbacks. Your unit can be a strength for the team, but also can lift up other units or positions on the team.

- Have a good grasp of life skills. They make eye contact with others, are on time for non-athletic appointments, have manners, etc.

MORE ASSORTED TIPS FOR ASSISTANT COACHES

- Understand and teach the game thoroughly. Know how to attack opponent weaknesses, win with the players you've got, teach fundamentals and research and teach the best drills to prepare your position group.

- Traits head coaches are looking for in assistant coaches: loyal, hard-working, reliable and trust-worthy. Being disloyal and untrustworthy are career-killers.

- Not everyone on the staff will get along—there will always be jealousy, personal differences, age differences but in order to win you must be able to put that aside to work with each other!

- Coaching is a family—build your network. Outside of your head-to-head competitions, consider other coaches as your co-workers, not enemies. Build a strong network. You will rely on them heavily throughout career. Keep it professional and courteous.

- Best way to move up from where you are today into a new position? Be the best at your current position! Treat your role and current school as your dream job, and work like it's where you've always dreamed to be.

- Your players will mirror you. You want them to do it right and pay attention to detail—you must take the lead and see that you take the little details serious, too. Do what you say you will do. Follow through!

- Your days will be unpredictable, you may get a surprise visit from the Athletic Director, a top recruit, the University president or a big booster... you just never know who you'll cross paths with. Dress daily in a professional way—always clean, crisp and professional. It's always a great idea to keep a spare suit coat, tie, dress, dress shoes and any other "church clothes" essentials that you can change into quickly if needed, to save time from running home.

- It's never "I," "me" or "mine." Instead, use "we," "us," and "our."

- No detail is too minor for the head coach. If they want to be kept up-to-date on an issue, keep them in constant communication with a quick text, call or email. It's better to over communicate than to leave them in the dark with your progress.

- Become a great evaluator of talent—you need to learn how to find the hidden gems who aren't gracing every recruiting Top 100 list. You need to be able to "find" great players before every other coach.

- Remember—you are ALWAYS representing your boss and university. Don't lose your job because you can't handle your alcohol out in public, get arrested or get into altercations. Like you probably warn your players, be careful of the company you keep as well!

- Understand and value that EVERYONE in the program has a role. Everyone has different strengths, everyone can contribute something different and critical: coaches, players, trainers, doctors, academic counselors, marketing staff, interns, students, boosters, maintenance staff, housing staff. Know people by name.

- Think ahead, anticipate what's next. What will your head coach need today/this week/next week?

- Self-evaluate and scout your team and position group. What weaknesses are returning? Evaluate top teams at those skills—how and why are they successful? What do they do exceptionally better? What drills can you use to help your players improve? Be brutally honest with yourself on which weaknesses your players need to improve on. Build on what they are really good at, show them how to get better!

- Nothing is beneath you—all hands on deck. Be wise with your time and put most urgent priorities first! Whatever is most important to your head coach is most important to you!

- Appearance is also important. Your days will be long, stress will be high—being in shape will help you fight mental and physical battles. Be well groomed, well dressed and energetic.

- How can you separate yourself—what value can you add to a staff? What can you become the best at, something they will be dependent on? Scouting, recruiting, relationships with prep coaches, developing players, leadership?

- Scout opponents as if your job depends on it—at some point, it will! The smallest of details can make the biggest of difference when it comes to game planning and having your players prepared.

- If needed, help communicate for your head coach. You may have to return calls for them, take on delegated responsibilities. Remember—your job is to make their job easier and to make them look good. Ask if there is anything you can take off their plate, as long as you can handle your regular responsibilities.

- If you lack experience or talent, you can overcome your weaknesses by being hardest worker who brings relentless energy—in the same way that you teach your players that "Hard work beats talent when talent doesn't work hard." Be the first coach in and the last to leave, and be the most efficient and productive during those hours!

- Be who you are and believe in who you work for.

- Never doubt the head coach in front of players or other members of the staff. When the negative talk begins internally everyone's job is in trouble. If there is an issue with the head coach, approach them directly and privately.

- Develop a good relationship with your player's parents—communicate! They need to be your allies, not your enemies! Deal with issues before they become unmanageable.

- Have a 'no gossip' policy with your spouse. Like you tell your players, 'What happens in the lockerroom stays in the lockerroom.' If they can't keep issues quiet, limit what you share with them.

- Answer the phone at any time, unless previously approved by head coach for a vacation or personal time.

- Carry yourself with a sense of urgency every day – at practices and meetings, not just for games

- Expect your players to be alert in meetings – feet on the floor, paying attention.

- Be consistent when discipline players. You can't hold your best players to lower standards that you hold every other player to, it's the first step to losing control of your team.

CHAPTER #13
ADVICE FOR GRAD ASSISTANTS

"Success is like anything worthwhile. It has a price. You have to pay the price to win and you have to pay the price to get to the point where success is possible. Most important, you must pay the price to stay there."
-VINCE LOMBARDI

"If you don't have time to do it right, when will you have time to do it over?"
-JOHN WOODEN

"No leader succeeds on his own."
-JOHN C. MAXWELL

"Become the kind of leader that people would follow voluntarily, even if you had no title or position."
-BRIAN TRACY

TIPS FOR GRAD ASSISTANTS AND INTERNS: LISTEN TO RECRUITING CALLS

I've learned from some of the best recruiters in the country. Each year there were some coaches who could sign nearly every player they pursued and other coaches who came up short every year.

Great recruiters are on the phone 24/7! Any time outside of practice or meetings—they're on the phone. They're pacing the hallways, on the treadmill, making a sandwich, watching video—all talking and talking and talking.

When possible, and without being a stalker, shadow these type of coaches to pick up patterns of what they talk about, how they talk to players and parents and how they wrap up calls.

What I've learned is that the best recruiters can talk to anyone at any time about anything, all while just being themselves. They can blend into any situation, walk into home visits or gyms from Hollywood to Iowa to Miami Beach to the bible belt of North Carolina to Brooklyn to Chinatown to Houston to Salt Lake City and blend in like the favorite family cousin.

This type of strength is something that must be mastered. For most coaches, it's learned.

Young coaches—or those looking to climb ranks and build their recruiting skills – listen to the best recruiting coaches on staff. Listen to their endless phone calls. Listen to them during Unofficial and Official visits. Take notes. Listen to how they start the conversations, what questions they ask, their tone, ways they sell their program, their personality, how they ask the tough questions, how they break bad news, how they wrap up conversations.

Oftentimes, they will make back-to-back-to-back-to-back-to-back-to-back-to-back-to-back-to-back-to-back-to-back-to-back-to-back calls, often with similar scripts. If you don't have a place to listen near their offices, listen on bus trips, car trips, waiting at the airport, after games. The best recruiters are endlessly on the phone. These are the coaches to shadow, conversation is an art!

MORE TIPS FOR GRAD ASSISTANTS AND INTERNS

- INVEST all of your time as a grad assistant or new coach. Be "the guy" or ("the woman") who is always there. Even if there is nothing to do in the office, there is always SOMETHING to do. Coaches work 24/7/365 so if you are always around, they will begin to include you in more and more projects. The more dependable you are, the more projects you will be involved in, the more responsibility you will earn and the more likely you will be promoted or recommended for other jobs down the road.

- Work at other university camps if your head coach and schedule allows. It's always good to expand your network, see how other coaches operate, work with new groups of players. Reach out to former teammates or coaches in your circle to inquire about working their university camps.

- In the offseason ask more experienced coaches you've worked with for advice. Don't turn it into an interview, stick to one question and keep questions generic. The point is to LISTEN—"What's the most important thing about recruiting?" "Best teaching points to use with players?" "Best ball handling drill?" "What are the keys to being a good talent evaluator?" Ask for a few pointers, and let them lead the conversation. See where the conversation takes you, you could pick up a few great lessons if you take the time to ask, listen and learn.

- Coaches are ALWAYS watching what you do, who you are friends with, how you carry yourself, how you interact with people, if you are punctual, if you delegate everything, your attitude—inside and outside of the facility. They may not call you out on it or even be coaches that you interact with or speak too, but know that they are always sizing you up and taking mental notes. Their opinions can help you or hurt you down the road with recommendations. Don't give them, or one of their contacts, a reason not to hire you!

- Help players at your position get extra position-specific work. Ask the starters if they want to take some extra reps, or offer to work with the backups, injured players and freshmen. Help your unit get stronger!

- Don't always be the one trying to get on camera—coaches know when you are going out of your way to do it, and it's obnoxious! Incidental camera time is fine, just don't jockey for it!

- Always bring a great attitude to work, even if you are having down days. Keep your personal issues to yourself, the team would never accomplish anything if every coach brought their personal issues to the office or complained about all of their problems. A drama-free personal life is important at this stage of your career, you won't have much time for a personal life.

- Think ahead, anticipate what's next. What will your coaches need today/this week/next week? It's always better to be prepared for a project that never comes, than to have an opportunity and not be prepared!

- You don't know everything! Be humble, be patient, be ready to work for it. Great coaching careers take a decade or more to build. You are in the position to learn. You don't need to prove or brag about your knowledge, instead focus on learning as much as you can!

- "This is how we did it at _____" doesn't usually go over very well with new bosses unless they ask for your suggestions. You are gaining key experience for the future, seeing how different coaches operate. Learn from their strengths and weaknesses, what works and what doesn't.

- Take the time to get your responsibilities and projects right. It doesn't have to be a race to get it done first, it's much better to get it accurate. If coaches have to always make you re-do things or double-check you all the time, that's not good and it will hold you back from future responsibilities and promotions, and a negative trait they will share with future employers with job recommendations. While coaches usually want everything yesterday, it's better to get it right than to get it done fast.

- Reward yourself a little! Have a balance, try to make some friends outside your office. Grad assistants or interns are often overworked, underpaid and have little free time—make sure to reward yourself on occasion for all the hard work you're putting in.

- Listen twice as much (or more) than you speak!

- Your days will be unpredictable… you just never know who you'll cross paths with. Dress daily in a professional way—always clean, crisp and professional. It's always a great idea to keep a spare tie, dress, dress shoes and any other "church clothes" essentials that you can change into quickly if needed, to save time from running home.

- As grad assistants or interns, yes, your job may unofficially include picking up dry cleaning, taking coaches on airport runs, picking up lunch, shuttling coaches' kids or wives around, house sitting or dog walking. Your job is to make your bosses' job easier, and by doing these non-coaching tasks you are freeing up their time and energy to focus on other more important responsibilities. My approach was to do whatever I could do to take off my coaches' plate, in order to free them up to watch extra film, game plan or call recruits.

- You have to adopt the "nothing is below me" approach. You may think you are being tested or handed busy work, but you aren't. A lot of tedious things must get done: class checks, envelope stuffing, ridiculous stat research—it's all important to your bosses and future references. Take it all on with enthusiasm and they'll entrust you with more.

- You need to have one of the best energies in the building—especially at practice and around players. You need to keep the atmosphere positive, relentless, energetic. Be yourself—don't force it—but be outwardly positive and energetic. Clap it up! Help keep the players relaxed.

- Be the first in, last out in the office. Nobody should beat you to work.

- With work, you earn two ways—money or experience. Experience will bring you money down the road, learn as much as possible, especially early in your career. Watch. Be there. Soak it in. Even if not involved, get a feel for what every coach and staff member on the team does. The linebacker coach doesn't only coach linebackers—they likely have academic, recruiting, housing, discipline, practice, budget, scheduling and/or equipment responsibilities. You aren't just learning the X's and O's, you are learning how a program operates. You are learning people-management skills.

- Coaching is teaching—so it's important to learn teaching methods. To be a great coach you must be a great TEACHER and tremendous communicator. Learn communication and teaching methods.

- Find a responsibility that you can call your own, no matter how tiny it may be. Treat it like a major responsibility, and work to become best in the nation or conference at it. Anything from cutting film, special teams, equipment, laundry, stuffing envelopes, airport runs... it's all critical.

- Don't drink with players or socialize where they party—it's not professional. You are not their friend, even though you are probably closer in age to them than your bosses. You are part of the coaching staff- act like it.

- Don't get drunk around your coaches, even if they do. You never want to say something or do something that can cost you your job, and it's much more likely to happen if you are getting drunk with your bosses.

- Be yourself! Know when to be serious and quiet, and when it's ok to show your personality. You are spending so many hours together, and coaches want to add great people to their staff- it's ok to have a sense of humor and personality.

- It's important—critical—to find any way possible to get involved in recruiting. You are limited what you can do with recruits as far as making calls or going out on the road, but there are other responsibilities within the operations of a team in terms of recruiting that you can bring value to.

- When recruits are on campus, realize that everyone in their circle is important. Treat their family, friends, coaches and any other visitors with them on campus in a first-class way. The coaching staff is not only building relationships with the recruit, but also with their entire circle.

- Help keep players loose, especially during intense times or losing streaks. There is a difference between horsing around and keeping players loose- know the difference. Keep them level headed, cut the tension and pressure and be positive, even in losing streaks. Help eliminate pressure off your players' shoulders so they play loose.

- Do not gossip! Other staffers or interns within the department will likely pump you for information... play stupid! One of the #1 things coaches look for is loyalty—what happens within the team stays within the team. Keep everything in-house—gossip spreads like wild fire and quickly gets traced back to you!

- Memorize the head coach's mission statement or core philosophy! Reinforce it with players, use the same terms or keywords that your head coach emphasizes. It's their plan, and your job to help turn into reality. You all have to share the same mission.

- Don't allow your players to be average. Encourage positive behavior: class attendance, grades, leadership roles, extra reps, focus, toughness! Even if you work only with the scout team—coach your players up! Act as if you are coaching the starters.

- Learn how to evaluate talent. Ask more experienced coaches (especially ones good at finding great, unheard of players) to sit in with them while they watch recruit video and ask for tips.

- Some of you may not be cut out to be coaches, and you'll figure that out within a year or two. Luckily, there are other opportunities within the sport-video, scouting department, recruiting, operations.

@1001RECRUITTIPS COACHES EDITION

ABOUT THE AUTHOR

The author has worked with over 70 NCAA Division I coaches over 15 years, including three "National Coach of the Year" honorees and 22 head coaches of eight different sports. Over the years, they have worked in eight different sports, alongside coaches and athletes, including over than 30 NFL, NBA, MLB 1st Round Draft Picks and several other players who have signed professional contracts. During that time, they were a part of #1 and #2 nationally ranked football classes, along with a Top 10 men's basketball class, as well as a BCS National Championship and an ACC Men's Basketball Championship. Throughout their career, they have worked alongside players and coaches who have won World Series Championships, Super Bowls, BCS National Championships, NCAA Men's Basketball Titles, NBA Championships, made Final Four Appearances and NFL Pro Bowls, along with individuals who have earned NFL Rookie of the Year honors, Heisman Trophies, National Coach of the Year honors, BCS Championship MVP Awards, NBA All-Stars, Cy Young Winners and both College and NFL Football Hall of Fame Inductees. The author, @1001RecruitTips has put together 'NCAA Recruit Tips' as your blueprint to improving your recruiting skills, combining these experiences for your guide to develop into the most successful coach that you can be!

MORE TIPS - STAY UPDATED!

Sign up for a premium "Coaches Corner" online subscription for just $9.99/month, with no monthly commitment at www.1001RecruitTips.com to help guide you to become an even better recruiter!

www.ingramcontent.com/pod-product-compliance
Lightning Source LLC
Chambersburg PA
CBHW070947180426
43194CB00041B/1646